Screaming Whispers

Charles Edington

AuthorHouse™
1663 Liberty Drive
Bloomington, IN 47403
www.authorhouse.com
Phone: 1-800-839-8640

Published by AuthorHouse 01/15/2015

ISBN: 978-1-4969-5793-1 (sc)
ISBN: 978-1-4969-6066-5 (e)

Library of Congress Control Number: 2014922713

Any people depicted in stock imagery provided by Thinkstock are models,
and such images are being used for illustrative purposes only.
Certain stock imagery © Thinkstock.

This book is printed on acid-free paper.

Because of the dynamic nature of the Internet, any web addresses or links contained in this book may have changed
since publication and may no longer be valid. The views expressed in this work are solely those of the author and do
not necessarily reflect the views of the publisher, and the publisher hereby disclaims any responsibility for them.

TABLE OF CONTENTS

FOREWORD

※━━━◆◆◆━━━※

THIS BOOK IS SPLIT INTO THREE DISTINCT AND DIFFERING PARTS, IT INITIALLY GIVE AN AUTOBIOGRAPHICAL SKETCH OF A BLACK MAN'S JOURNEY FROM POVERTY IN THE GHETTO TO A MENTALLY EMANCIPATED CITIZEN OF THE WORLD.

POEMS, POETRY AND DISCOURSE ON "HUMAN RELEVANCE" MAKE UP PART TWO.

PART THREE GIVES AN INSIGHT-FILLED "<u>PROFILE OF BLACK PEOPLE</u>" IN TWENTY-FIRST CENTURY AMERICA – STATISTICAL AND SOCIALOGICAL INFORMATION TO ENHANCE UNDERSTANDING AND HIGHLIGHT THE SOCIETAL IMPEDIMENTS A LARGE SEGMENT OF THE AMERICAN CITIZENTRY HAS TO OVERCOME REGARDLESS OF RACE, RELIGION OR FINANCIAL CIRCUMSTANCE.

SCREAMING WHISPERS

❧⟨⟩❧

Mighty Strident polices the world, and gathers abundance to go to the moon
But, sooner than later, the flag unfurls and its influence and might takes a worldwide swoon

Forty million without health care; twenty percent of Hispanic households earn less than $23,000 working the whole year
Eighty-seven percent minorities fill UP the prisons
So, the obvious conclusion is abundantly clear

Our over-taxed support soon starts to pale
But they say, our economy's highly at-risk, and these duping entities are "just to big to fail"

The "house" and the "senate" boast of a new non-partisanship
While the system's design suggests social welfare dominates, so why do they trip

How will we know when we've gone too far?
NINE hundred billion spread around so far,
And "big member" says they need government help selling us a car

"for the good of the country….. to protect the system", they say
but the "publicans" disagree, and many of the "r" people flatly refuse to play

what? Now the mother of all bailouts, seven hundred billion they seek
and, what's more they push an inattentive congress to get it done in a week

The Barbar Shop contingent, asks "did you see this $1.4 trillion stock market lost, done in just one day?
Former Emperor, Senior Twig, concludes this will look like "chump change" if we don't do it his way!

THIS TWO PARTY SYSTEM HAS AN EIGHT HUNDRED POUND GORILLA SITTING IN THE ROOM
AND, HE SAYS, I ALLOWED YOU NEARLY TEN YEARS OF UNABATED SPECULATION AND UNREGULATED BOOM

NOW, SOMEONE HAS TO PAY FOR THE $60 BILLION IN HEDGE FUND BONUSES, GOLDEN PARACHUTES, AND OBSCENE PAY RATES FOR THE MANY CEO'S NO TIME TO APOLOGIZE TO "JOE SIX-PACK", THE MARGINALIZED MINORITIES, OR ALL THOSE NEGATIVELY AFFECTED AS MIGHTY STRIDENT CONTINUES TO STEP ON THEIR TOES

AFFLUENCY SEEMS TO HAVE A CLICHÉ RESTRICTION AND IT'S PLAIN TO SEE THERE'S NO PLACE AT THE TOP FOR ALL THE POOR, DISENFRANCHISED FOLKS STRIVING TO BECOME ECONOMICALLY FREE.

APHORISMS 4U 2009

MEMO

<u>TO</u>:

THE MARGINALIZED MANY AND THE HEAVY LADEN

<u>FROM</u>:

SOLACE AND REAL STRENGTH

IT TAKES A VERY POWERFUL PERSON NOT TO ACT IMPULSIVELY AND GET PULLED DEEPER INTO A DISASTEROUS SITUATION. IT TAKES SELF COMPOSURE AND CALM JUDGEMENT NOT TO ANSWER FALSE ACCUSATIONS, NOT TO DEFEND AGAINST INJUSTICE, OR TO FEND WITH AN "EYE FOR AN EYE" MENTALITY.

BECAUSE TO THE INSTINCTIVE HUMAN PSYCHE NOT TO ACTIVELY DEFEND ONESELF AGAINST INJUSTICE IS CONSIDERED "PASSIVE"

NOTHING COULD BE FURTHER FROM THE TRUTH!

FATHER TIME

SCREAMING WHISPERS

PART – I

FORMATION OF A PLIANT WILL

―――――――――――――――――――――――――――――― ✦❖❖✦ ――――――――――――――――――――――――――――――

"It's too bad, youth is wasted on the young" some insightful scholar once remarked,

But, I was the exception, I enjoyed virtually every minute of my childhood. I tried new things, sought new places, and was usually characterized as a glutton for new knowledge, differing experiences, and novelty in general. Think how much more we would enjoy life if we maintain this appetite for novelty throughout our life.

At an early age, about eight or nine, I agreed with that often noted dictum, "money may not be the most important thing in the world......... but it was way ahead of whatever was in second place."

I decided, no, I vowed, not to be poor "when I grew up.

That done the course of my life was changed.

As an insightful guru once remarked, "Ain't nobody coming! If it is to be, it's up to me!"

So, I quickly determined that one of the keys to success in this dog eat dog society, was to have a good education. Minimum!!

I later also surmised at an early age, that it didn't necessarily matter what school you were "in", it was how much "schooling" got "in" you. I've met idiots from Stanford, and have been awe struck by Community College graduates.

Next, I concluded, if you do the things the way everyone else had done them, you will more than likely windup like everyone else: a "wage slave", working hard to eat, keep warm, and cover the expenses of working!!– To "exist" or "live"; only "to existence", this, I did not want!

An insightful quote often notes "We either better get busy living or get busy dying"

In most situations, I tried to "think outside the box!" to get off the "beaten track" And, to "search the circumstance" for the smartest solution. Avoiding the haphazard trial and error solution mode, I soon found that being in the "resolute decision" mode was tantamount to accepting a lonely vigil and doing most things alone. After all, if you've made up your mind….. from whom else do you need affirmation?

Why resolute? Because impulsive actions are usually so inefficient; costly in terms of time and resources; but, worst of all to me it was not an effective expedient toward resolution. Thus, action soon became a synonym for progress – after all, I couldn't keep my eye on the prize for extended periods of time (I might miss the opportunity to move up to the next level).

So, the next concession on my way to the "good life" was to choose a vocation or career that was not only rewarding mentally, challenging intellectually, but paid well.

That was a tall order, but for the next eight or ten years, I thought I had it solved when my older brother and I made a pact: He would be the Doctor, and I would be the Pharmacist – and we would then lock up a fair portion of the money in the area. Shows how naïve I was!

So, I jumped into "college prep" classes – math, chemistry, geometry, foreign languages, etc – in my quest to achieve what is called "sophisteration".

Things were easy, as I whizzed through High School with good grades. I joined the High School band, played first chair clarinet (My preference, playing drums was denied – full up!). I Enjoyed several years (three!) learning Spanish, earned a "school letter" as a member of the first Tennis Team. All, the while in High School, working a part-time job or two - Some times wrapping homemade candies, of peanut patties, peppermint sticks, taffy or brittles working at the Candy Shop. Or, working as a part time custodian at a nearby linen and uniform laundry company. – these teen jobs came in rapid succession after earning my stripes as a shoe shiner, paperboy, and just helping out at the one of the near home the cafes. Jobs in the ghetto were available, if the spirit was willing – the environment often contributed.

After what might be considered an industrious youthful period, the obstacle of college funding reared its ugly head.

I recall the critical choices that had to be made ….. even in economically inopportune times….This was one of my earlier encounters with a life changing situation I characterized as a visitation from "Major Jolt" (i.e. deciding to "go or stay", "play or pray", suffer or stuff-it, etc)

I knew in my final year of high school that my parents were not a financial resource! With six kids at home, and only Dad working on a post-war job at the Supply Warehousing Center, earning $80 dollars a week. It just couldn't happen!

I was born just after the "Great Depression" in the worst possible social climate for Black people. Racism was virtually institutionalized. Voting, in many southern states was subject to a "grand parent" voting prerequisite, eating establishments often evidence signage of "White Only" not just on the restrooms or water faucets but to enter the establishment! Income levels among persons of color were meager and sorely lacking.

These circumstances prompted a mass migration from the South to the West and the Mid-west. With the coincidence of what has historically been characterized as the "World War II" era. Employment, forced up by the War, for the thousands of voluntarily displaced Black families was magically improved and became an added inducement and a means to escape the barely livable income levels found throughout the "deep south".

WHO ARE YOU?

My family, the was among those who fled the destitution and poverty of rural Arkansas, as did many other Blacks from southern states, to the "promised land" of the west.

The patriarch of my family and the father of fourteen kids took the "leap of faith" and relocated to the marginalized area on the west coast. There, he took the only job he ever had in a structured work environment as a warehouseman. There he worked for nearly forty years essentially in the same position with barely enough income to support the many "stair-stepped" children he spawned (approx one year to one and a half years apart); including two sets of twins, and three dead before they were thirty.)

Dad lived his Baptist religion to the hilt. He never drank or smoked; why he wouldn't even stop at the liquor store (and Lord knows there were plenty of them in our neighborhood) to buy bread – for fear of being seen in the store and having it misconstrued!

I was born the fifth oldest among the clan; and, from an early age my parents stressed "education, education, and education" laced with a liberal dose of "good, ole time religion". This was my father's prescriptive panacea for riches and mental well-being. Pop was always known to say, "as long as you live under my roof, you'll go to church every Sunday morning for Sunday school, later church service, and return in the evening for "B.Y.P.U" (Baptist Young People's (training) Union)

Mom was a quiet dutiful wife. She shunned excesses of any sort, and never showed disagreement with Dad's edicts or decisions. And, most knew who the (behind the scene) resolute leader of the family really was – none other than this seemingly quiet little lady of the house.

Several unfortunate mishaps occurred during our many years in the ghetto, Little Sista, at twelve years old stepped on a rusty nail while crossing an empty lot and subsequently died of "lockjaw", the colloquial name for Tetanus infection. My brother, Jr, while playing in the neighborhood streets, at age eleven, was hit by a car and was hurled approx twenty feet in the air and landing nearly under the wheels of another oncoming car – only to suffer minor bruises and the lost of a couple of dislodged front teeth.

Miraculously he was quickly restored to health. He was so impressed with the demeanor and skills of the emergency room physician, while being treated for the bruises sustained, that he found his "calling", and went on to become an orthopedic surgeon.

In retrospect, his revelation illustrates that, situations, though often unexpected, which appear to be foreboding or injurious, often times, through the grace of God, are turn into fortuitous or major milestones for good.

Grandma used to say, "God can make a straight lick, with a crooked stick" Isn't it amazing how intelligent the old folks become in retrospect, as you get older!

It seems, I began working just after grammar school. I built a shoe shine box, and walked to the nearby public places to shine shoes for a pittance (or it seemed as such!). Later, I wrapped candy, as noted before.

I happily kept a Paper route seemingly forever, and my last adolescence stab at joining the workforce was as an after-school part-time custodian. I had no fear or reservations about working because Pop employed an "effective work incentive" program of giving each of the six to eight kids at home the unenviable sum of a quarter a week for allowance!

In the summer, most of us caught the "picking" bus at daybreak in the morning to ride for what seem to be hours to what we called the "agricultural belt" area to join our Hispanic brethren as farm laborers – picking beans at one dollar a box, or "topping" unions at a dime a pound, or (my favorite) picking peaches for a few pennies a lug.

This work served two purposes: It allowed us to bring home bags or jackets full of whatever we picked, and it served to keep a few dollars in our pockets and enjoy the feeling of "helping" the family economically to "make-it".

This "help" also extended to periodically jumping over the local Dairy Creamery fence after they loaded the delivery trucks with eggs, milk, butter and other "dairy necessities" – these, we liberated in the spirit of re-distributing the wealth.

The railroad yard within walking distance of the house, also proved to be a veritable ground-swell of goodies with the nearby freight cars loaded with canned goods, manufactured items and other "household" necessities.

But, so much for misspent youth!

With a family of our size, there were always plenty of people in and out of the house and many friends, relatives and onlookers nearby. For the kids in the neighborhood, our house was the favorite huddling place, across from nearby playground.

One day after playing basketball with the "neighborhood bunch", we started talking about life after High School.

At this time in the evolution of the black American male, 1957, the options most of us knew were: to try and get a job at the Post Office, go into Military service, or live by your wits as a marginalized "criminal" in dope dealing, pimping or other unsavory lifestyle choices. All of which had little or no appeal. The "Group" and I, in our naiveté considered illegal activity "too sorted and risky". And, this fear was reinforced in each of our psyche, to a man, because we were afraid of going to jail. We called it "The Bubba Syndrome" Who wants to be "up close and personal" with Bubba?

We decided on Military Service

I remember, we all got excited about seeing the world, while we gained "G.I. Benefits" of a subsidy for college or trade school. And, subsequently we would become eligible to buy a home with nothing down - not to mention the mystical lure of being able to go to foreign countries we had only read about. The sign of the times historically was that Black males had serious problems getting "good" jobs, and most usually concluded that the military service was their best option toward achieving at least a "taste of the good life".

One insightful person once remarked, that during the fifties, sixties, seventies and even the eighties, Blacks filled up the prisons, the military, and the ranks of the under-employed. Three Strikes!!

The neighborhood clan further narrowed our military choice to the "Buddy Plan". This Military plan would allow us to go into the Service and stay together (we thought).

Also, we thought, it would allow us to learn an employable trade (touted in Army commercials), save some money, and gain acceptance into a society which continued to demonstrate it institutionalized hostilities toward people of color.

THE AWAKENING

Later in the summer, several of us took off on a Saturday morning on a "gambling lark". We loaded into one of the brother's car with a hastily contrived plan to drive to Nevada "stateline".

W e stopped to eat at an ironically named little town called Hangtown.

Having lived rather sheltered lives in the marginalized ghetto, we were less than naïve, so we sauntered into what we called a "greasy spoon" eatery "en masse", and walked directly to a booth and sat down.

We sat for a while. watched the waitress whisper something to the cash register guy, who walked into the rear kitchen area; only to quickly emerge with a second guy who looked like a wrestler and he wore a tall white cook hat, we thought it only natural that he, the cook, was holding a butcher knife in his hand.

The stereotyped wrestler-type walked straight to our table, and with the bravado of an arrogant cop plurted: "You boys can have anything you want To Go! But, you can't eat in here!

We looked at each other in disbelief. And finally, somebody said, "Is this what discrimination feels like?" The answer was a resounding Yes!

So in characteristic fashion, we first huddled-up to weigh our options, and with heightened bravado, we decided to play their game.

We got up and stood as a group by the front takeout register area, and waited for the waitress to take our "to go" selections. We gave the charade a look of realism by appearing to carefully study the menu.

We ordered three sandwiches for every two people, replete with sodas or milk shakes, fries, onion rings and wedges of pie all around.

We waited until twelve minutes had past, when we were sure the cooking, cutting and packaging were well underway – Then, we simply got up and walked out, "leaving them holding the bag", so to speak.

That indelible incident left its mark on my psyche, and I decided then and there, I would not risk my life in the Military to defend the rights of an intolerant populus which were allowed to discriminate at will without consequences.

After all, this was 1957!!

So, a self-assessment was in order, I had taken most of the right High School classes. I had, as they say matriculated in pre-pharmacy.("Matriculated"….matriculate! - if you do you'll clean it up!)

I had under my belt, algebra, analytic geometry, chemistry, three years of Spanish, English lit, and even the three years of school band - as first chair clarinet, I thought I was ready for U.C. Berkeley.

Unfortunately, after pouring over the University catalog, and laboriously figuring out the best class schedule, my application letter was rejected – close, but no cigar!

Hey, I didn't have the money anyway, I rationalized.

Undaunted, I decided to go to the local community college, and get an Associate of Arts two-year degree, then go on to a four year university.

So I started transferable undergrad classes like Chem 1A, 1B, Calculus, French, Zoology, and the like - with a math-science (pre-pharmacy) major objective..

Meanwhile, my social life of non-stop weekend partying, drinking and "chasing skirts" took a turn for the worst.

The shapely and petite, cute little thing, I called "my girl" informed me, in the vernacular of the neighborhood bunch, that "grandma didn't come last month."

In other words, she missed her period, and she was pregnant!

Being the nice guy that I am, I couldn't bring myself to ask, "whose is it??"

So, I seriously started to study, Chem. 1A, French, and Zoology. But, as fate would have it......... things again took an unanticipated turn. Enter my old friend Major Jolt!

My pregnant girl friend calls one night, out of the blue, and tells me her finance, was coming home from the army on leave and she wouldn't see me until he returns to the base after the holidays.

The weight had been lifted!

My wanderlust continued, I started dating what I considered to be a safe, church-going, sweet, naïve, young lady from a nearby town.

My community college student career (and I do mean "career"…three years at a two year institution) was going along fine when all of a sudden "major jolt" reared his ugly head again

My former lady friend brought a paternity suit against me.

My new lady announced that she too had caught the "nine month disease".

Woe is me! Oh woe!!

I decided to get another viewpoint, so I drove over to my old buddy's, house to try and discuss my options with him.

When I arrived, there was a loud argument going on in the living room.

It seemed that my timing was atrocious, for I had interrupted a planning meeting of a black liberation group. I joined in the discussion, but it seemed my proper english and my continued demands for more detail immediately alienated me from the group.

After a couple of thinly veiled threats to "kick my ass", I was politely asked to leave.

I didn't mind leaving, but my feelings were hurt when they called me a "bourse house nigger".

So, that night, I had to confer with my personal "leadership forum": Kentucky Tavern (straight bourbon), Panama Red (weed), and that stellar fellow, "Historical Recall"

And, after several hours of serious meditation and insight, I concluded that my best option was to marry this lady I loved, get a job, and work college in as the opportunity availed itself.

"NONE OF US HAVE IT ALL TOGETHER
BUT TOGETHER, WE CAN HAVE IT ALL!"

THE STREETS ARE SAFE, HE GOT MARRIED!

Employment has always come easily to me. (Thank God!)

Once the decision was made, I quickly passed the Postal exam to work full-time from 5:00 a.m. to 2:30 p.m. and obtained a second full-time position as a chemical Laboratory Technician with graveyard hours from 4:00 p.m. to midnight. After all, I had an Associate of Arts degree in math-science, so there!

Who needs sleep, now that I was anticipating two kids, and a new bride to support.

So, I married in September with $14. "to my name".

But, by the holidays, at yearend, I had accumulated, as a result of working two jobs, a small amount of savings. I was also living now in a neat new apartment building with my young, pregnant wife – I was determined to make this work!

My sweet petite former girl friend, decided to play hard ball, when she heard I was married and she sued for increased monthly child support

When the judge literally "dropped the hammer" on me with a court order of three hundred and fifty dollars a month child support, I was flabbergasted! The judge really got my attention when he countered my argument with, "True, you're a student, but you can pay it, you got potential!" (When you have no power base or advocacy "They" can do you any way they want!)

Number one son was born, to my former petite lady, and a few months after I got married, my new bride and I were blessed with little Jr, the following May.

Two kids! A wife! Child support! Incomplete education! Not the recipe for disaster, as many would imagine, but "raison d'etre" as the French would say. So, time to get busy, I told myself.

Awesome responsibilities, with endless decisions interposed themselves in my life. All of which required constant judgement and choices. But, I remained determined to make it work and hold it all together.

LIFE GET'S GOOD'ER

In the ensuing months, we were able to find a clerical job for the new wife. Meanwhile, I quit the post office job, and enrolled in the local University. I began working only the graveyard shift as a Lab Technician. The job was a godsend. It enabled me to complete my lab work in about five or six hours and study for the remainder of my unsupervised nightshift.

At the University, I selected business as a major and soon earned a bachelor's degree in Accounting with a minor in Business Administration.

Still, I was anxious to earn money and create choices, so after learning that the only requirement for a real estate agent's license was to be able to "fog a mirror", and be at least eighteen years of age; pay the fees and pass a "multiple guess" test with 70% or better.

This I did in short order and started to investigate avenues for making money.

At that time, the Housing Development Federal office offered a program for low-income folk to purchase property of from one to four units, as their personal residence, with as little as 3% down. (Note: This percentage by some quirk of circumstance exactly equaled the commission paid to the Buyer's real estate broker). Hence, I had to become a Broker, not just an Agent.

This too was fairly easy, since any Agent who had a four year degree and basic coursework in real estate "practice', "finance", "law" and "principles" (Only a "Pass – Fail" grade requirement) would qualify.

Most of the courses tied in with my major and recent coursework at the University, so within a few months I became a State certified Real Estate Broker.

I was now ready to "make my fortune"

I quickly bought a four-plex apartment with little or nothing down and delayed the first month's mortgage payment for 45 days to collect a month's rents. (I offered more than the seller's asking price – and then had the seller pay all of the closing costs) This turned an immediate ongoing profit, so I bought two more houses: both with similar financing and little or no funds out of pocket.

Now, armed with rental income, and a fairly impressive balance sheet, I was ready to make some "real money".

But, as fate would have it, ole "Major Jolt" reared his ugly head once again to shake my "comfort zone".. This time under my own roof!

It seemed that my wife, of tender years, in the course of her employment at the army recruiting center had become infatuated with a certain Sergeant there.

Given my suspicious nature and the unerring logic that the "mind demands order" I soon confronted her about her "goings and comings" and we separated shortly thereafter.

Now some friends of mine, when they broke up with their intended lifelong mate would go into a "malaise" depressive state and for an indefinite time become dysfunctional and trash their life. I decided "none of that for me", so I quickly found a replacement in "sweet Susie". Now Susie was built like the proverbial brick **# house, and as Marvin Gaye use to sing, "she sho liked to ball!!

Susie seemingly was a "trusting soul" (who gave you your space); and, was a stable working lady. Her endearing grace was that she was very caring and always made sure we had all of the creature comforts and constant entertainment…jazz, dining out, theatre, and the necessary lifestyle entrapments of city life. It seemed to be working out fairly well so, we rented a small flat in the City and we moved in together..

She had a "shop-a-holic's" mentality with exquisite tastes and I thought that was a pleasant change, being pampered and having a seemingly loyal ……… to a fault, lady.

In short, Susie was "good people", and the timing couldn't have been better!.

Life was great! One had many options from which to choose. The "metro" as we called it had a wide selection of eating spots, couched in a constantly changing entertainment and community activities landscape….all readily available…. If you have the money!

Imagine paying ten to twenty dollars for a half hour's parking, or buying a pair of Italy imported shoes at $300 to $1400… while selective folk could at the same good time by going downtown Brisket & Beef Steak House and get a freshly char-broiled steak dinner and salad for about nine dollars with your own bottle of Vino De Tavola wine! Life was good!

So, I continued to dabble in real estate, I hung my license with one of the oldest intown realtors, Tokada Realty. And, already being a Broker, I didn't have to waste time going through their in-house training and orientation. In short, my time was my own.

I happened across a nice house on the Avenues that was an easy "fixer", so I bought it, in my favorite way, with my commission, under the same "home development" little money down, program.

I remodeled the house upstairs with an "avant guard" antique pink fireplace, new carpet throughout, and new appliances.

The downstairs basement I converted into a third bedroom, with a den and bar. I even put the television and a fish tank in the wall which separated the rooms, so that only the glass would show. I had installed a plush deep pile carpet, and built-in mirrored shelves behind the bar, and triumphantly dubbed the downstairs parlor, the "Sin Den"

At this juncture, I was somewhat distrustful of females, and I decided to become a free-wheeling bachelor. I built a crap table with a green felt layout I bought in the City, and had poker chips made with the insignia "Sin Den" prominently displayed on top.

I was now ready, I figured, for my new lifestyle.

After a long exchange with Sweet Susie, I move back across the Bay (alone) into my newly decorated house.

I soon organized a semi-monthly poker game on the weekends closest to the 1st & 15th of each month. As the "House Man" (owner-manager) of the game I "raked" or cut the pots 10%, in exchange for providing free fried chicken, potato salad, soda, hard liquor and beer or comparable fare ranging from barbeque, fried fish, poor boy sandwiches, etc.

Sin Den took off big time! The place had a good reputation as "an honest game", friendly limits, and plenty of new card decks (to control or counter claims of cheating).

Since there were so many eligible men in and out of the place, and the local chatter about my antiqued pink fireplace with its palm trees, plus a full bar downstairs, soon groups of ladies started to come by and have a drink or go upstairs and play music and dance.

Needless to say, the money poured in – the 10% rake from every pot averaged over $40 an hour. Since the games started on Friday around 7 p.m. and usually continued non-stop until early Sunday morning, I became a pawn shop, loan shark, match maker, and a poker croupier. And, between the pawned watches, rings, guns and loans, I became a man of means with leisure time.

I became more than a little self-indulgent, and tried on the "playboy" role. I bought a 240Z sports car, bought more property, and started hanging out at the jazz clubs in the City. This is the era when real jazz was in vogue, so I and my most recent friend would chase good entertainment up and down the west coast..

Life was good!

When things were slow, I would drive up to Lake Tahoe for a quick turn of the dice and horseracing with or without a new found lady-friend.

I often found myself taking dates to the best Area restaurants, or just taking a leisure drive up the coast to Santa Cruz or Monterey for dinner and a walk along the beach.

I enjoyed refuting the notion that "hard work" and planning was the sure way to a successful life. I was, what my ghetto buddies called, "nigger rich".

Unfortunately, I paid an all too often visit to the hospital emergency clinic, for the three hour investment of time to get STD - venereal shots. I often thank God that HIV and Aids was not rampant during these years.

MENTAL DAZE, OR EDUCATION CRAZE?

One day, an old friend, and I were "just hanging out" and we started to talk about the "state of affairs" of Black people.

"Hey man, guess where I was last night?". I said

Before he could answer, I interjected, I was over at the Civic Center at a "speak-a-tron" featuring Martin Luther King, Mohammad Ali, and Angela Davis.'

"Can you believe, in 1963, Congress is in the third week of a filibuster to block the

Civil Rights Act. And, according to Martin Luther King, our President, Lyndon Bains Johnson, is going to ignore the smear tactics of Hoover at the FBI!"

"I'm not surprised, he muttered. "These devils "got us" lock, stock, and barrel under their thumb."

"You saw what happen to the Liberation group. They dogged them out so bad that some had to go to get out of the country, in exile"

"And don't forget the kid who was only about seventeen when he was riddled with bullets by the police", he countered.

"Yeah", I said, as I thought about the black man's plight in what has been characterized by some as, "these yet to be United - Snakes of America"

"This town is over fifty percent Black and about four hundred thousand people strong. Don't you think we ought to be able to do something about the condition of Black people?" I said, without really expecting an answer.

"Hey man, I was planning to go to the mosque tomorrow night, why don't we go together?

"What's it like", I asked

"Minister Raja X, really has something to say to Black people. But, I don't want to spoil it for you, let's just go and see how you feel afterward.

"OK, I'll try it, I said

Now the Black Muslims had the respect of many during the seventies and eighties. The Brothers were thought of as a dedicated group of Black men who were, as it was often put, "Nation Building".

The self-discipline was quickly noted, and the men always wore a suit and tie, and were clean shaven and acted very resolute and decisive.

The women, when you saw them, were usually with a man and usually had their heads covered and wore long dresses and no makeup.

The men were referred to as "The Fruit of Islam" or "FOI" and as an act of obedience and humility personally sold the "Mohammad Speaks" newspaper, one paper at a time, daily!. My first visit to the Mosque was enlightening,

I came without a jacket, but was not allowed to enter unless I put on the borrowed coat pro-offered by the men who greeted you at the entrance with a friendly, "Ai salaam ai lakum" (peace be unto you).

The seating was separate for the men on one side of the building and the women on the other, with guards surrounding the stage.

The head of the Mosque was introduced, as Minister Raja X. He took over the meeting by lecturing on the plight of the Black man and treatment he received from the "white devils, here in the wilderness of north America."

He easily depicted the typical black man as either a "negro" characterized by low self esteem, no power base and generally having few choices in the selection of a noble path for his life.

On the other hand, the Black Muslim who had been given the "knowledge of self" knew his history and had been given the moving descriptive horrors of the slave kidnapping. Also, as Minister X was often quoted as saying, Black people suffered through a hundred plus years of slavery while working from "can't see in the morning til can't see at night.".

Then, after being lawfully deemed "chattel" or property, not human, released in 1865, only to fall prey again to a share-cropping system of utilizing borrowed resources controlled by the plantation owner and damned to a life of endless debt.

And, in the 1970's and 1980's when finishing even high school was accomplished by less than fifty percent of the eligible, the alternative for sparely existent employment was to join a segregated or discriminating military service, or wind up in jail. It was rare for a high school dropout to obtain a "decent job".

One pretty much had to agree, the deck was definitely "stacked" against the Black man.

So, he then posed the question, "what are you going to do about it?"

The men joined in large numbers, pledged to support an organization owned and operated by the Black man............. The Nation of Islam headed by Elijah Mohammad.

Minister Raja X, a self-professed former dope-head and homeless wanderer who was now in his last year of medical school, lectured on "How to Eat, to Live"

I was impressed, and the many instances of racism and institutionalized shunning of Blacks became readily apparent and clearly seen.

The fact that local city had over fifty percent Black population and had few black officers, but recruited its police from the South, requiring only an eight grade education confirmed a lot in my mind..

The fact that at that time, few if any blacks worked in city hall, especially in accounting and administrative positions provided even more confirming evidence, especially after I applied for an accounting clerk job and was given a test which was harder than any college entrance exam – but you never got to know the questions you missed. They simple told you your score and that you would be placed on a list for approx one year.

That familiar, old saw, "Don't call us, we'll call you!"

One didn't have to look far, to easily see the many instances of bias, segregation or rank racism.

What incensed me more than the obvious were subtle things as the news media, movies and television characterizations of Black Men. They usually put the camera nearly up their nose to accentuate the thick lips, uneven teeth, or bad skin – all designed to make the viewer see someone repulsive and not "like them", therefore, it was OK to treat the race as less than equals.

Yes, it didn't take much to see the relevance of what the Black Muslims were teaching.

With a new resolve, I made a covenant with myself - to take better stock and to become much more sensitive and aware of what, where, and how, I utilized my "time, talent, and treasure."

I became much more pensive and less impulsive with my life and meanderings. I reviewed in my mind my current status and experiences.

I pondered:

Here am I, born the fifth oldest of fourteen children to parents who had approximately eight to ten years of structured education between them. The major adventure of my parents was that they had not remained in rural South during the Depression and War years of the late nineteen thirties and forties. My father was a God-fearing Black Man who had seen his grandfather killed by a hostile mob, as an "arrogant uppity nigger", they said. And, my mother's father died at an early age in a little shanty town where the only doctor (who was white) made a mistake in removing his appendix and sliced his liver in half. And, the kids in the family heard the often recounted story of our grandfather saying to the doctor, as he bled to death, "well doc, looks like <u>we</u> made a mistake this time!"

I empathized, at the time, with the outspoken Barbara shop philosopher that said, that he would never be seen eating watermelon, and that he would never downplay his intelligence or do "mental buck dancing" and act like a foot shuffling nigger no matter who were his audience.

Longfellow's poem became my new mantra, "We must make our lives sublime, and leave footprints on the sands of Time"

I sought to get more involved with Black people and lend my talents to the betterment of the race and forsake my current selfish lifestyle of "Me, me, My, my, Mine".

"NO CPA LICENSE FOR YOU BLACK SUPPORTER"

LIFE AS WE KNOW IT

〜⚬×‖×⚬〜

I met with, a "fraternity brother of my older brother, and I agreed to take over the accounting and reporting for Liberation movement fund.

The tasks were simple and intermittent. I would record the income from around the country, and record the expenditures for legal and attorney fees, travel, etc.

This lasted for approx a little over one year. When the leader was acquitted and returned to college to continue his studies, the Fund was discontinued.

Several odd happenings occurred during this short accounting assignment. One day I received a letter from the United States Treasury Department indicating that I had been selected for an interview for a position as a Treasury Agent.

The odd thing about this was, I had never applied for such a position!

But, my curiosity was peaked, and I wanted to see what this was all about, so I responded that I wanted to interview. My thinking of course was that the interview would be conducted in the Federal Building. But, to my surprise, the response came back, almost instantly, indicating that they wanted to conduct an interview at my home! I agreed.

It turned out to be a farce of course. The interviewing "officer" turned out to be a middle-aged Black Man with a conservative look and an obvious interest in everything except my credentials to do the job. It put me in remembrance of something Minister X had said, "remember, "House Niggers" ride shotgun even better than the white boss."

Or, Malcolm's story about the difference between the plantation slave that worked in the "big house" versus the "field nigger"............ when the plantation boss didn't feel well, the House slave would say, "what's the matter boss, we sick?

After about an hour of personal history questions and wandering conversations about my interests and recent activities, it was clear to me this was no job interview. So I looked the so-called interviewer in the eye and said, "I don't feel I would be comfortable acting as a bodyguard for foreign and U.S. dignitaries, and walk along side their limo as a protecting policeman." This ended the interview.

I attended the Mosque frequently for a while, but was not accepted by the brothers. It seemed my grammar, or stilted English, and my lack of a testimony from the streets was again my undoing. So, I soon stopped going.

14

I decided to go to work. My sister, Nadine said she had recently done some temporary work for a Black-owned grant technical assistance firm which was looking for an Accountant.

She said, "If you're interested, I can hook you up!"

The timing was perfect. I had done a lot of soul-searching and decided that if I didn't go into business for myself, I would prefer to work for a Black organization. But, during this period, I had been wrestling with an even bigger challenge, whether or not to marry this cute little girl I had been seeing and had even taken to the Mosque. She was a true "soulmate", smart, perceptive and caring.

So I interviewed for the Controller's job with the consulting firm and after securing the job, we drove to Nevada and got married. I felt no pressure. We worked out a plan for her to continue College and I would also pursue a Master's degree with evening and weekend classes at the University.

I started my work at the Consulting firm.

The rigors of the job were challenging, and very satisfying. My only regret was that so much money (from "cost reimbursement contracts") was being passed around and not enough was stopping at my door!

So, one day while on a trip to Washington D. C. attending a subcontractor site visit with the President of the company, the subcontractor proposed a "partnership" co-venture in handling a major portion of the funds available on a grant.

Now the President had an advanced degree in Public Administration and I had just finished my third master's degree class in Business Law and he had just a few weeks earlier dissuaded me from taking a leave of absence when I got accepted into U.C.L.A Law School by doubling my salary if I agreed to wait one year.

So, the stage was set for me to demonstrate my knowledge regarding business law considerations as they related to a "partnership

We stayed in Washington D.C. for several days hammering out the agreement terms, but I think the firm President was impressed when I indicated in the middle of a meeting that the essence of a joint venture partnership absent clear language to the contrary in the written agreement would leave the courts to construe that each of the parties if sued could be sued "jointly" or severally (individually) at the election of the plaintiff. And, my insistence that we obtain adequate insurances and structure clearly defined reporting avenues for "transparency" undoubtedly won him over to trust my judgement and he was assured that I had his interest at heart.

I thus had the Controller position as long as I wanted it.

Later, during this period, I wrote an outline for the firm President's approval to start a travel agency. The many traveling Consultants working a myriad of contracts were now averaging over twenty thousand dollars per month in travel expense. And, the typical margin on travel was easily over eighteen percent. This proved to be a tidy annual profit.

We also managed to increase the profitability of the firm and my stay there was both challenging and rewarding.

The money was very good there and I stayed in the position for longer than the one year promised.

After getting the Master's Degree in Accounting, and the consulting business started to reflect the lessening of government grants for job training, education, and labor placements. I decided to join the ranks of corporate America.

Through a combination of restlessness caused by the clear insight as to how Black people were treated in the ole U.S. of A, and the feeling that somehow life was passing me by, I subconsciously started a period of what I characterize as "wonderlust". I became bored after a couple of years with conventional lifestyles and seemingly repetitive daily habits of eating by my watch, three times a day; eat ….sleep….work….only to repeat the cycle, "ad nauseum". Work…. to pay bills, maintain an expending posture of indebtedness which required you to continue working. Change was not an option – conventional justification was: support your family, pay for the car or furniture, or the house. Accept the taking of only two weeks off per year for vacation from work - but stay within budget constraints or go nowhere at all. In short, I had become, what I had dreaded most of my life, a "Wage Slave".

So, without specific planning, I tried taking an accounting job with the newly initiated "Poverty Program", in one of its funded nonprofit entities, the Social Services Corporation.

It felt good to interact with black folk again!

I set up the accounting procedures, wrote the corporate personnel benefits offered, negotiated the business insurances, assisted in the structuring of the various programs offered: Emergency Assistance Resource, Indigent holiday grocery give-a-ways, Intake and Referral to other City program entities for housing, substance abuse, job training, and the whole gambit necessary to address the myriad of misery measures facing the marginalized, institutionally ostracized, and many times "unwise" acts of the city residents.

The Director, was offered a better job, with higher pay and benefits, and he resign without notice. So,, after we had just obtained stability and internal efficiency in the newly formed nonprofit corporation. I stroked my ego, and volunteered to handle both positions, as Controller and Director for the remaining seven months of the funding year.

I immediately started working on writing the "Three Year Plan", because we had been informed by the city oversight agency that the Social Services Corp. was to be the lead agency in the planned Citizen's Center.

After many long hours of research, outlining and subsequently writing out a comprehensive plan of operation and administration, the document of approximately two hundred pages was accepted by the community Board of Directors, and the City Department.

I saw an opportunity to make these temporarily funded offerings of the programs self –supporting and possibly become "institutions" of indeterminate life.

What I placed in the Plan was funding format such that the approximately two dozen agencies funded by these Federal funds could take twenty percent as an additional charge for "labor fringe benefits". This, I thought should not be far fetched, since the City's total fringe benefits rate was well over seventy percent of the labor costs

Thus, of all direct labor (personnel costs), there would be a requested reimbursement of twenty percent to place with a fiduciary agency called the Western Model Fund

The Western Model Fund, of course, was my invention. And, with the help of an insightful insurance Broker, we had projected that the layers of income expected over the next five years would put the Fund in control of hundreds of thousands of dollars. And to start it off, I started placing the twenty percent of labor costs from my corporation into the Fund.

In less than a quarter, the accumulated funds grew to over fifteen thousand dollars.

The "cost reimbursement contract" simply had to be supported with an invoice and an agreement – both of which I designed and instituted as part of the semi-monthly funding requests to the City.

When I started to discuss the possibility of the other, twenty or so, agencies joining the Fund, and the structuring a rotating Investment Board of Directors, from among the various corporate officers, somehow the City got wind of the "goings on" and called me on the carpet to explain fully what was involved.

Upon threat of bringing fraudulent and/or embezzlement charges against me, I was made to cease and desist from further funding transfers and to return the proceeds of the Fund back to the City.

I was flabbergasted and disappointed; there was no deleterious intent on my part. So, I had to "cool my heels" and go back to conventional wage-slave mentality.

However, about this time, the sexy little secretary, who had worked so closely with me on developing the Plan, Verna, suggested we have a drink after work and "co-miserate".

She didn't have a car. She suggested we ride together.

Additionally, "why waste money on bar drinks", she intimated.

She had an apartment nearby, and she lived alone. Let's go to her place, we agreed.

Well, as the guys used to say, "Push came to Shove", and I wound up spending the night.

Infidelity – can be shortened to "infidel". Marriage can be shortened to "marred".

.And, lastly, trust can be shortened to "separation". The trilogy started that night, and ran its course by my moving in with my newly found "roll mate". But, after a few weeks, I realized what a selfish short-sighted mistake I had made.

When the "dust had cleared", along with my head, I interviewed with a local Certified Public Accounting firm and soon thereafter was hired as a Staff Accountant-Auditor.

After auditing on many jobs of many national corporations, and nonprofits and private businesses, I grew enormously in the accounting, fiscal, auditing world both professionally and personally. I decided to make "bean counting" my career, profession, and mission in life

After working with over two dozen new hires at the once prestigious Certified Public Accountants "par excellente", and sitting for the state CPA exam twice, I was not able to pass all four parts with a score over seventy-five percent. My nemesis was "Accounting Theory", I could only get a score of sixty-eight percent. Sixty-eight percent was the highest score given without passing.

I was determined, so I took a Review Course and tried again.

Again, sixty-eight percent, something was amiss!

Working with the CPA firm was good exposure, but I soon grew tired of being billed at $225 an hour and getting paid $20 an hour. The exposure and career growth was great, but I also knew that contemporary "Big 8" public accounting firms operated under an unwritten historical law of "No Black Partners", so I decided to move on.

I alerted the firm's placement officer of my intention to leave and he indicated he could easily place me with one of the firm's clients or associate organizations. However, I was startled to hear him say at the exit interview, "good luck, we hate to lose you, you know we only have three blacks in the firm, and you've been doing good work, and we had plans for you.....you were one of the blacks that could talk" (i.e. properly use the King's English!)

I was placed with Nationwide Stores, Inc., as one of their Corporate Auditors.

The job was to audit whole "Divisions" of stores – from Los Angeles with over 200 stores to Alaska with only a hand full of stores. The Company would rent an apartment for the Auditor and his family and additionally pay a travel allowance of approx $135 per day plus salary, and all of the living expenses – such as utilities, rent, parking and mileage.

The job was great! I could save my complete paycheck. And, with little effort, I could also bank part of the travel allowance.

Within less than two years, I saved over eighty thousand dollars.

I did not simply save the money in a bank account, I invested it with the local stock brokerage company in preferred high dividend stocks and bonds. I took it a step further and put the savings into a "margin account" in which one could borrow up to 50% against fully paid securities. So, I invest 150% overall in such securities as PG&E, Occidental Petroleum, Kansas City Pwr & Light, and other high-yield securities. I paid 5% to 6% interest on the twenty to thirty thousand dollars I constantly had on "margin" – But, I received an overall return of 7% to 11% on invested funds. While monthly putting into the account approx $4000, the margin balance with dividends, market price increases, new fund infusions allowed me to accumulate over $80,000 with roughly $11,000 in investment earnings.

So, after division audits in Fremont, Los Angeles, San Francisco, Long Beach, and Seattle, I quit!

My security broker, Hal, had arranged for an interview with the firm as a Security Analyst (Stockbroker). And, I made the job transition without a break in employment.

The "broker-age", as the guys affectionately referred to the firm, would pay a salary for up to three years after sending new hires to New York for five weeks of training and licensing, and then local training and help so that one could develop a clientele.

The job was a "fun time" in my life. After spending the weeks in New York, at company expense, studying and seeing all of the top Broadway live plays, I returned to the local office where I worked from 7:00 a.m. until 1:30 in the afternoon, the remainder of the day was my own. It only sounds as if I was a "slacker"! The truth of the matter is, I produced more new clients than virtually all of the fourteen other new brokers.

But, unfortunately my name did not end in "i" or "o" like the favored new hires who got the best of the "call-in's" or were assigned as "floor brokers" during the heavy traffic hours. Note: The Office Manager was Italian American, who took good care of his own, and most of the new hires knew who would get the "gravy referrals" as we call them, while the remaining new people fought over the "crumbs".

But still, I managed to hold my own with new accounts, reachable calls and overall sales.

However, it didn't take a rocket scientist to see, that it if you were to make approx fifty-one thousand a year, in commissions income per year at an approx three percent rate, one would have to sell in excess of $1.7 million dollars in securities per year.

So, at the end of the salary years, I felt it was time to move on and take the resume benefits of having been a stockbroker.

I later learned that, apparently the State Board of Accountancy did not confine their score-giving to just examination answers. Later court disclosured, and it was admitted by The State Board of Accountancy that they had discriminated against Filipinos for a period of nearly twenty years. And, by way of correction, they would allow any failing former applicant to simply take a business law class and they would be certified. Life goes on!

I had seen the "profit maximizers up close and personal" so I decided to "job-hop" for the next few years, to expand my horizons and ward off the boredom of repetitive humdrum work.

The plan worked to perfection, I "bounced" from job-to-job for more years than I care to say.

I held a litany of positions in the ensuing years; positions as Corporate Auditor for National Stores, Stockbroker, Accounting Manager, County Accountant, Financial Accounting Supervisor, Sr City Auditor, etc. – all with different entities, none for more than four years.

Meanwhile, the clock was ticking and time it was a passing – so, one day, I said to my self: "Self, you know you're getting older and you need something to carry you through your "old age" (that mystical apprehensive period when people think they will run out of money, choices, and family-support). And, thereafter they would have no choice but to accept a lifestyle which represents a "giant step" backwards).

I then decided that under the "tier I" retirement plan for the State, I could retire at fifty years of age, and also choose to take social security in advance until age sixty-two; then, at sixty-two I could take the social security and a reduced pension from the state. A great plan, but in came my old friend, "Major Jolt". It seemed that the current baby's mama I was living with had developed a gambling problem. She would take a bus to Reno or Tahoe on Friday evening, and I wouldn't see her again until Sunday. Of course, the many checks and charge card costs would follow her down the mountain – thus crippling our financial and emotional situation.

The divorce cost me half my pension, so I had to put more emphasis on the real estate side of the income equation. I half-heartedly thought about working again.

I knew that most jobs only require approximately thirty to sixty percent of your effort to satisfy the mandates of the employer, so I started to actively return to real estate even after reaching fifty years of age with only one or two more years to work.

I bought a "fixer" four-plex, and transferred to the local Services Dept. in the same city – There, I planned to retire and work the social security advance and state pension for a "cushion" of approximately two thousand dollars per month. This amount, I thought should allow me to dabble in real estate and with rental income to supplement my needs. I should be alright. This sounded good, since I thought I would still be young enough to enjoy life with travel, leisure time and just "kick back".

HABLA USTED ESPANOL?

While I was living the laid back life of a divorcee in my four-plex, my older brother ("Doc") suggested I accompany him to Hondurus for a couple of weeks.

He had married, a cute, petite, intelligent lady who was a native of Tele, Hondurus.

It sounded good to me since I had taken three years of Spanish and thought it a good diversion from the seemingly endless remodeling I had undertaken on the four-plex.

The remodeling was finally finished and the units were all rented....so I was free to "roam" again.

Hondurus is a small Central American country of less than eight million people with extremely high unemployment and an unbelievably low per capita income.....In short, most of the citizens were "dirt poor". But, much to my surprise I found the people almost oblivious to racism and prideful attitudes. I rarely encountered begging or stealing, but I found that the people took more than a casual interest in those around them and offered help when needed.

I noted that a large American export corporation had somehow owned or controlled most of the banana fields and pineapple plantations and paid laughable wages to "los povrecitos" hired for little pay and worsening living conditions. I often heard the story about the workers in the small town of Tele who rebelled against the exporter and set fire to the shipping dock in protest.

There were many interesting things to see and do in Hondurus. So, for the next two years or so, I would fly to Houston for the three hour lay-over and then on to Hondurus.

I became known as the single American, and soon I was getting marriage proposals and friendly greetings from the pretty senoritas – most of whom were half my age.

I spent several evenings in the disco bar and lapping up the local favorite, tequila and beer chasers.

One night I happen to see a dark skinned lady with beguiling eyes and asked her name. I was told her name was Maria and later I was told that she was single and wanted to meet me. That was the beginning of a long relationship which took me literally all over Hondurus to the towns of La Cieba, San Pedro Sula, Teguchigalpa, and of course my local haunt of Tela. I had a decent nest-egg of savings, so I decided to buy a huge lot and build a tourist resort. After all, Tela had the most beautiful beaches in Central America.

I bought a lot which was one hundred sixty feet wide and over nearly two hundred feed deep, for about twenty-seven thousand dollars. Then I built a two bedroom house on one end of the lot and planned to retire in Hondurus with my dark-skinned beauty, the surprisingly industrious lady, Maria.

Now Maria worked as manager of a small pizzeria. The rub was that she worked six days a week from ten in the morning until the six or seven p.m. evening closing. This put a crimp in my time with her, so I had her to quit and show me Hondurus.

We spent quite a bit of time at the many beaches or at the large central market place where I often bought a whole two to three pound fish and fresh veggies for three or four dollars. We would cook it in the kitchen of the hotel suite I rented for twenty-five dollars a day or we would travel to other surrounding cities and eat at the best restaurants where the check was rarely over eight dollars.

Bernardo, Maria's father was a carpenter, so I asked him to estimate the cost of a small American "tourists compound" or resort. I planned to invite Americans over to vacation in Tela, Hondurus. Bernardo suggested I first build a wall around the lot which I thought was a great idea, so I hired him to do it.

The lesson I learned from "Hondurus construction projects" was that the key man can support his whole "down line of relatives" once he gets control of the purse-strings!

Needless to say, several cousins and friends suddenly showed up on the weekly payroll as cement mason, painters, brick-layers, etc.

In short, the ten foot high wall of approximately three hundred and forty feet long, cost me more than the seventeen thousand dollar house I had already built in. But, I rationalized, the "compound" was completed and now I was ready to build bungalows, sun decks, barbeque pits and spa settings – not previously seen in this part of Hondurus. And, to offer this "piece of paradise" to what I thought were hundreds (maybe even hundred of thousands) of naïve American "wage-slaves" who had no idea what life in Central American could offer them. I would introduce the neophyte tourists to the indigenous "garaphuna". – the direct descendents of the slaves that were brought out of Africa, but were left all along the slave ship routes of central and south American shores. The garaphuna Africans maintained their classic black features of extreme dark skin, wooly hair, and tribal customs. They fished, early morning or at night, and the women sold the fish in the huge market town square. A five to seven pound freshly caught fish could cost you all of three dollars. Why, you could feed the whole neighborhood for less than ten dollars..........which in fact, I often did. This generosity brought me several marriage proposals and unfortunately the label as the "nice, rich American". Thank God for a sister-in-law who was a native "Hondurena" and could advise and help me avoid some of the pitfalls of daily life in Central America.

Gossip in the homes was the main source of news, no daily newspaper or local television,

It never ceased to amaze me, some of the happenings that transpired.

Roberto, the dark-skinned "money changer (favored by our group) was threatened "by the competition" or other money-changers in town. But Roberto was defiance and "his-own-man" so to speak. So he ignored the threats, and got himself a couple of large dogs to guard his house. The "competitors" got past his safeguards and managed to "shot up" his house. He escaped with only minor injuries in that instance.

But, I was saddened to learn, a couple of months later, that Roberto had been killed, by "parties unknown". A strange but beautiful county, I thought.

I soon learned that the American dollar was a much sought after commodity in Hondurus. I found that fourteen or fifteen "limperas" (the Hondurus dollar) was the equivalent of one U.S. dollar, and the banks would pay approximately 5% to 6% interest (in limperas) on U.S. dollar deposits. So..... after a little math calculation, I deposited a few thousand U. S. dollars to earn approximately, two thousand limperas per annum, payable in quarterly increments. This income I then planned to use as my travel money when I journeyed in and out of the country. The plan was working beautifully, until my little "dark-haired honey", Maria, decided to purchase a fourteen hundred limpera refrigerator with the bank surplus deposits. So much for "unpatrioted surplus funds overseas!" I scraped the plan and closed the account.

So, life in Honduras was slow but satisfying. To travel up and down the Honduran costal area to San Pedro Sula, La Cieba, and "Teguchigalpa... finding new beaches, and waterways of Waynaha and all the while living on less money than you could ever imagine, I felt it was a great! But, after a few weeks, I started to get "homesick" for the good ole "U.S. of A". So, I decided to come home for a while.

As fate would have it I arrive just in time for a celebration party at my older brother's house. My brother, by now, was well established as a practicing and I must say sought after orthopedic surgeon in the local area.

After clipping along on a meager income of over three hundred thousand per year, he had acquired a 6600 square foot home .... And, I can always count on him to say, "Not bad.... For a poor boy from the west-side ghetto, heh!

Well, as I entered the house filled with the aroma of fresh food and baked goods, a quaint little lady caught my eye. As our stares met she smiled sweetly and said in a soft voice.

"So you're the globe hopping travel brother?

I replied, "I don't know what they told you, but only the good part is true!"

This was the start of an evening of conversation and pleasant interaction.

And, as the night wore on, I got to know Andalene fairly well and we planned lunch the next day. Andalene was different from ladies I had known in the past and I was frankly intrigued and curious. She had worked for some time and had her own place and appeared to be very self proficient and independent minded. This was good!.

We dated often and dined at the better restaurants around the coast, and we often hung out at the Chez Louie's. for drinks and conversation. She was active in a long standing Baptist Church, and she struck me as an all around good person. I soon met the family and made fewer and fewer trips to Hondurus.

One day in Hondurus, I had a serious talk with my Central American honey, Maria.

I said, "how would you like to come with me, with your two young daughters to America?"

She looked at me pensively and said, "I thought you were going to build a tourist compound, and stay here in Hondurus!"

Why can't we do both, I have a four-plex in Berkeley with plenty of room for the family, and we can fly back and forth as needed to manage our new tourist vacation resort." I replied.

She smiled sweetly and said, "why don't we think about it and talk more later"

Well, I thought, that was that. After all, as the brotheran would say, "the boy is green as a pool table and twice as square!!"

As time wore on I made fewer and fewer trips to Hondurus, and spent more time with Andalene.

In fact, I joined the Baptist church, and volunteered to assist in the preparation of the church budget and financial reports. After all, I had this Masters degree in accounting and Public Administration…. Why not put it to good use!

And, as fate would have it (or better yet, as God ordained it) I decided Hondurus was not the life for me, and I proposed marriage to my new found soulmate.

And, of course, in fairness to Maria, I gave her the construction project in Hondurus… including the house and the recently-built two-car garage and by then, the 700 feet of nine foot high walled-in enclosure. So I turned the page on that period of my life and redirected my attention to the country of my origin……the good ole U. S. A.!

The bible tells us, "it is not good that man should be alone", so I invested some serious time in my newly found soul-mate, Andalene. On my last trip to Hondurus, I knew I would not be coming back when I found myself all nervous and "hyper" about going home. I could hardly wait to get back to Califonia, and I found myself picturing a life with Andalene; so I called from the airport and asked Andalene to be my wife. She graciously consented, and we started planning a big wedding in her long attended Baptist church.

So, for the next few months, we shopped for a house planned a fifteen person wedding ceremony with dual ministers, replete with food and dancing and many gifts. It was great!

I quickly sold my four-plex in Berkeley, and we bought a seriously under-priced home in the bedroom community near Napa valley.

I started to volunteer to do accounting and budgeting work in the church, and soon learn that the business of saving souls can be as demanding as corporate life in administrative needs and expenditure controls.

Now the pastor of the church, Reverend Leroy and several community-minded individuals had incorporated and purchased a community-based conference center. The facility was called the Hills View Conference Center, and could be rented for events, such as weddings, birthday parties, banquets, and all sorts of group activities. The hourly rental rate was low, and the facility had a modern kitchen, and enough tables, chairs, and electronic equipment to accommodate groups up to twelve hundred people in it's banquet hall. The problem was, the facility income would not support itself to include the monthly mortgage, utility costs, maintenance, and staffing needs to make it a viable business.

As fate would have it, the Mayor, often dubbed the "politician's politician" and affectionately referred to by folks in the City as "Da Maya".

I had personally followed his two to three decade career in the legislature and his public appearances around the area with great admiration and respect. Another coincidence and happen stance I noted, we now attended the same Baptist church! In fact, the pastor, Reverend Leroy, had been appointed to complete a City counsel position by Da Maya, just a few months earlier and they were close friends.

Andalene and I were asked to become the Directors of the Conference Center at a very friendly salary. We gladly accepted and started the eighteen month revitalization of the landmark.

We lowered the rates, included our chef at reasonable prices for a wide array of "soul food" specialties and upgraded the appearance of the building and interior. We leased the lower floors to permanent monthly tenants, and started an upgraded daycare (leased to a city agency). And, in just a few weeks, the Center became the pride of the community and more importantly, solvent and self-sufficient!

PEARLS

When one has the perceptive abilities to look at life from the perspective of the disenfranchised, institutionally biased posture of the black man in this wilderness of north America, its easy to retrieve, surmise and philosophically wax eloquent on the historical, cultural, and obstinate lack of a moral compass which characterizes the societal mores of the country's leadership. Now, after seventy-five years of living in what I characterize as "mental subjugation" where the black man must not only be twice as good as his competitive peers, but must also "scrape and bow" with "Amos-n-Andy" reverence and deference to the orders of the dominate class in all but his often limited "super private" circumstance.

The televised and widely circulated quotes of an N.B.A.'s owner, in describing how he feeds, pays, and generally, "takes good care of his negras" was shown as outrageous and had "no place in the twenty-first century"

But, at the same instance, on another television channel, a governor says, "Blacks were better off in slavery, they worked, were feed, and didn't have to worry about a place to live.." How hypocritical is that!

In an era when four hundred Americans have more than the combined wealth of one hundred and fifty million citizens; and, two-thirds of the workforce in the country earn less than fifty-four thousand dollars a year – It's no longer a "racial" struggle, but a "class" struggle in which the under- represented minorities and marginalized many are subsumed into one large segment of the population regardless of nationality or race.

Meanwhile, the corporate-financed legislature continually propose funding cuts, elimination, or setting "sunset" limits (five years on Welfare maximum) on the "wage-slave" populous. Fifty separate votes to eliminate subsidies for old age (social security) or medical attention for those who can ill afford a four thousand dollar a day hospital bill The list is almost endless.... Student loan obligations with no jobs available, lengthy ruminations and delays voting to extend unemployment insurance… I.R.S. pulling the certification of nonprofits (for not filing within the last three years – even though, only certified last year!!). You have but to look at the news and the story behind the news to ask, "Who is suppose to regulate or have the oversight responsibility for correction and prosecution of these things?

One insightful Wall Street Baron recently said, "It's when the poor slobs can't feed their families, in large enough numbers, that the real civil fighting will start. Right now, it's only isolated individuals going "postal" or cracking under the strain of feeling helpless, and seeing the obvious exploitation by those supposedly put in place to help"

As a former President, recently said, the republicans have their way for a while and when situations or circumstances pull the covers off their national or major exploitation of the citizens, they are voted out and the democrats come in.

What he failed to say is that this time they have gone too far and may have ruined major components of society, such as housing, employment, major industries like banking, auto manufacturing, education thru onerous student loans with no jobs at the end of massive debt.... and the list goes on!

But, this time its different, as one minister puts it, "The abomination in the sight of God.... Has been transformed into an Obama-Nation, with the help of God".

CLOSING NOTE

It's not enough to "lay bare" the gravity and magnitude of the societal "sore" now pervasive in America, or to "comiscerate" and dwell on the maladies we face everyday without at least suggesting a plausible and enduring solution.

Also, let me remind readers that this country was literally founded on religious precepts and a steadfast belief in God. Virtually all of our doctrines, articles, and Constitution are filled with language which pre-supposes divine guidance and an abiding faith in a higher power than man.

We now need biblical direction more than ever!!

The true and biblical notion of "church" as an integral social institution suggests that we use the concept of a "body of Christ", which mandates a sense of "unity" and "oneness" regardless of denomination or name. The Catholic, Presbyterian, Baptist, Lutheran, Mormon, Jesuit, and the nearly endless continuum of "fractionated units" which comprise the most segregated Sunday groupings in society should be dubbed "hypocritical". The Bible refers to "believers" as belonging to the "Body of Christ" not the Baptist Body, or the Lutheran Body, etc...... further, the biblical quote of Jesus directs that "If <u>my people, who are call by my name</u> would humble themselves and pray, and seek my face, then will they hear from heaven and I will "heal the land".

POEMS, APHORISMS, & MEANDERINGS

PART – II

Poems, aphorisms & meanderings

Table of contents

LIFE SHAPING PRAYER

*LORD…GRANT ME THE HUMILITY TO ACCEPT
THE THINGS I CANNOT CHANGE*

*GRANT ME THE AMBITION TO CHANGE FOR THE BETTER THE THINGS THAT
I CAN CHANGE*

GIVE ME THE SPIRIT-DRIVEN WISDOM …..TO KNOW THE DIFFERENCE!

"THE FEAR OF GOD…. IS THE BEGINNING OF WISDOM"

APHORISMS4U

HEALTHY, WEALTHY, & OTHERWISE

ATTRACTIVE STICKS OF STARCH WITH NO NUTRITIONAL WORTH
DEEP FRIED IN GREASE, HEAVILY SALTED…THUS, THE FRENCH FRY IS GIVEN
BIRTH

ONE HUNDRED SEVENTY POUNDS OF SUGAR WE EACH YEARLY CONSUME
WE SUBSCRIBE TO THE "BIGGER SHIRT" THEORY WHILE WE CONTINUE TO
HIDE FROM THE EXERCISE ROOM

NOW MEDICOS PREDICT ONE CHILD IN THREE WILL BE PLAGUED WITH
DIABETES
BUT, WE CONTINUE TO IGNORE THIS, BUT SOMEBODY OUGHT TO SEE
WHILE THE GOLDEN ARCH'S SELLS ITS SEVENTY BILLIONTH BURGER, NOW
USERED UP WITH A NEW EXTRA "SWEET TEA"

NOW, TWENTY FOUR MILLION DECLARED DIABETICS,
WHAT WILL IT TAKE TO OPEN OUR EYES
WHY MUST WE CONTINUE THIS FANTASY AND LIVE OTHER THAN WISE

NEUROPATHY, BLINDNESS, NEUTRALIZED EXTREMITIES AND FREQUENT
EMERGENCY CARE
SOME TRY TO EAT KOSHER, OR USE DETRIMENTAL DIETS, WHILE PRODUCERS,
RETAILERS, AND A CONDESCENDING GOVERNMENT CONTINUE TO SHRUG OFF
THESE FACTS AND LEAVE US UNAWARE

FIVE HUNDRED "QUICK STOPS" PLACED IN JAPAN… THAT DON'T SELL GAS!
THEY PUSH 99 CENT HOT DOGS WITH SWEETENED DRINKS, HOW LONG DO
YOU THINK THEIR CULTURE WILL LAST?

SOON 1.3 BILLION CHINESE WILL GAIN ACCESS AS WELL
AS WE EXPORT THIS HEALTH HAZARD, TO ENHANCE PROFITS, AND LET THEM
CHOKE ON ITS HELL

ADDED NOW IS A NEW MALADY, "DI0-BESITY" WHERE DIABETES JOINS WITH
GROSSLY OVERWEIGHT BODIES TO FURTHER PLAGUE OUR LIVES
DEMANDING A NEW REGIMENT OF EXPENSES, STRONGER MENTAL HEALTH,
AND GREATER COMMITMENT FROM CAREGIVING HUSBANDS AND WIVES

SO THE WAGE-SLAVES VOTE FOR OFFERED POOR CHOICES

BUYING INTO THE DEMOCRATIZED SHAM THAT THEY REFLECT OUR TRUE VOICES

SOME ASK, "HOW WILL WE KNOW WHEN WE'VE GONE TOO FAR? THERE IS NO CURE FOR THIS HIGHLY COMPLEX DISEASE!
WILL WE CONSTRUCT ANOTHER "BAILOUT" WHEN THE INSURING HEALTH MAGNATES YELL, "SOMEBODY HELP US, HELP US PLEASES…!

APHORISMS4U

WHO KNOWS THE MAN IN THE BOX

The smell of lilac and fresh flowers shrouded inside an organ music background
Low murmuring conversations and sad solemn faces all around

To pay our respects and show that we cared
Relatives, friends, and acquaintances all go marching by the Box, to take a quick stare

Austere, a "loner", "slightly off", or other aptly applied phrases
He lived his whole life in many personally selected stages

But, who really knows this Man in the Box?

He dabbled at business, He regularly played church
But what was his true nature? What attitudes, inclinations, or proclivities were last or first?

Friendly, and Giving, to a fault
Never settling….what he wanted, he bought!

A wizard with few resources, and always ready to advise
How he lived on "social insecurity" and a gas-bill pension, suggests that he was truly money-wise

But, again….who really knows this Man in the Box?

Cliches, aphorisms, limericks, or other mantras were his short answer in most situations – it depended
on just how he happened to feel
His favorite diatribe was "Time wounds all heels!"

Alone, but not lonely, he was always quick to have something to say
He warned aging wage-slaves to start spending, to travel, or just to "find a new way"

Body was too old for working, and the forfeited contest between food or sex
Though the memories were sweet
He would instigate a stimulating verbal exchange, or offer up a quick, "let's get something to eat"

So, slow in motion, but always suggesting new ways for life to be unlocked
He even wondered, who really knows the Man in the box

Many thought him old fashion, old Christian… with a weakness for Chance
Some thought, he still had his wits about him, but just too old to dance!

But, with business, investments, real estate, and the like
He'd help you for little and often for nothing, and suggest new ways to make your dilemma a change
of direction in your life

But, that wage-slave mentality soon put his suggestions on the shelf
Thus, conventional thinking soon took it's toll, and that habitual problem kept repeating itself

Children now grown and mostly gone, setting their own pace
Oft times having a new ideas, but without the wherewithal to put them in place

Alas, time became the enemy, and vexed both body and limb
Still the boy held on pretty good......walking tall, trying to look active and slim

His End was swift and without agonizing delay
Thus, we still picture him vibrant and active, he wanted it that way

So, take heed you slaves of habit, with short-sighted goals
Age is not the enemy, it's your thinking that's old

Thus, when life's aspirations and loss youthful ambition get's you stuck in a lock
Remember that ever active mindset and zesty enthusiasm shown by this Man in the box.

APHORISMS4U

TRUTH

YE SHALL KNOW THE TRUTH, AND THE TRUTH SHALL SET YOU FREE!"

IF YOU CAN ENVISION "TRUTH" AS THE ULTIMATE EMBODIMENT OF ALL THINGS; OR, WE CAN THINK OF IT AS THE ESSENCE (HIGHEST AND BEST) LEVEL OF COMPLETENESS.

IT'S THEN NOT TOO FAR FETCHED TO SAY, THIS CONSUMMATE STATE OF ESSENCE WILL EXIST AS A SOLE AND SEPARATE AMALGUM WHICH WOULD "BE" IN PLACE EVEN IF NO ONE KNEW ALL OF IT OR UTILIZED IT.

THOUGH IT IS ELUSIVE AND NOT A SUCCINCT HYPOTHETICAL SUMMATION IT WOULD IN EFFECT BE THE ONLY COMPLETE AND FULL ANSWER TO "ALL"

SO, LET US EXAMINE THIS THEORUM IN TERMS OF ITS ATTRIBUTES:

*IT WOULD BE ONLY ONE OF A KIND

* IT WOULD BE THE PENULTIMATE ANSWER TO EVERYTHING

* IT WOULD BE THE FINAL RESPONSE FOR THE OBJECTIVE MIND. THE ELUSIVE "LINE" BETWEEN THE MATERIAL AND THE SPIRITUAL COULD THEN FOSTER AND REFLECT A WIDE DIVERSITY OF MAN'S "LOGIC DEMAND" AND MEANDERINGS IN RESPONSE TO QUESTIONS …SUCH AS… "WHY AM I HERE?"," WHAT IS THE PURPOSE OF LIFE".."IS THIS JOURNEY ALL ABOUT ME ONLY?".."WHAT MORAL IMPERATIVES (EXISTENCE GUIDELINE) SHOULD I ADOPT?"

HOW WE ANSWER THESE QUESTIONS, OF COURSE LEADS US TO "RELIGION"

* IT WOULD BE SO FAR AHEAD THAT IT COULD BE DUBBED A DEITY OR GOD!

NOW, LET US EXAMINE "MAN" (ANTHROPOLOGICALLY SPEAKING, "MANKIND "): INSTINCTIVELY, HE IS SELF-CENTERED, SELFISH AND IF "CHANGE" OCCURS, IT HAS TO BE "LEARNED".

THUS, IF WE ARE MOVING ALONG "A CONTINUUM OF LEARNING "GROWTH", OUR IMAGINATION, ABSTRACT THOUGHT AND CREATIVITY WILL PAVE THE WAY FOR THIS TRUTH "LEARNING PROCESS" TO BECOME IMBEDDED IN OUR PSYCHE.

IF WE DEFINE "RELIGION AS THE EMBODIMENT OF A SERIES OF DOCTRINAL BELIFS THAT UNDERGIRDS OUR PRIMAL MOTIVATIONS AND SELF ACCEPTANCE, THIS SERVES AS A "MORAL COMPASS" FOR OUR DECISIONS, ACTIONS, AND REMEDIES TO RESOLVE LIFE'S CONCERNS.

EGO – SIN – TRICK

ARE YOU SELFISH, SHORT-SIGHTED, AND CHEAP?
YOU DON'T HAVE A CLUE ABOUT WHAT PEOPLE THINK OF ABOUT YOU
AND, YOU AIN'T TO PARTICULAR ABOUT THE COMPANY YOU KEEP!

VOID OF EMPATHY AND NOT TOO LIBERAL WITH YOUR SYMPATHY AS YOU
ADVISE YOUR BROTHERS TO "MOVE ON"

BUT SOON LIFE DEALS YOU A BLOW, THAT WE'VE ALL COME TO KNOW – WHEN
YOUR CHARISMA AND BRASSINESS IS GONE!

AND, IN THAT TERRIBLE DAY YOU DON'T KNOW WHAT TO SAY, AS THE
REALIZATION COMES TO YOU THAT YOUR NATURE AND SELF-IMAGE IS WRONG

SO YOU DIG DEEP INTO YOUR MENTAL BREECHES LOOKING AT BUSTED
PERSONALITY STITCHES AND KNOW THAT ITS TIME TO CHANGE

BUT SOMHOW YOU RESIST YET GIVE IN TO YOUR WISHES THAT A NEW WAY IS
NOT AS FAR-FETCHED OR STRANGE

BUT, WHAT WAY SHOULD IT BE, SINCE PAST SELF-CENTERED THINKING ALWAYS
REVOLVED AROUND "MY STUFF, MY MIND, AND ME"

SURELY THERE'S HELP IN THE "GOOD BOOK" ON THE SHELF, AND I CAN FIND
DIFFERENT WAYS TO INTROSPECTIVELY SEE

AH! THERE IT IS! I FOUND SOLACE IN PHILIPPIANS 2:3
"DO NOTHING OUT OF SELFISH AMBITION OR VAIN CONCEIT, BUT IN
HUMILITY, CONSIDER OTHERS BETTER THAN SELF"

EDINGTON'S APHORISMS

I'S JUS B' TWEEN POSITIONS

SEEMS I WAS BORN OUT HER' IN DES STREETS
I SEEN JUS ABOUT EV'A SCAM WURK'D, AN' SOME CAN BE AWFUL SWEET
I SEEN ALL THE ADDICTIONS YOU EV'A WONT'S TO SEE
WHY, I SEEN 'EM SO HIGH, THEY COULDN'T EV'N SEE ME
SO, WHY DO I KEEP DO'IN THE THANGS THAT I DO?
YEAH! I KNOW YA WONTS TO KNOW, SO I'LL ASK IT FUR YOU
WEll, IT'S A LONG STORY, BUT THE PUNCH-LINE IS SHORT
I'M JUS ONE OF DEM "NO-NECKS" THAT FELL CLEAN THRU THE CRACKS
YEAH! JUS ANOTHER TWELVE YEAR OLE IN A FORTY YEAR BODY
MY DADDY'S SOMEWHERE'S OUT DEY; PO MAMA JUS COULDN'T COPE
SO I TRIED TO MAKE IT INA CRAZY WORL WITH THE HEP OF JUS A LITTLE BIT
A DOPE
AND DAT'S WHERE IT STARTED, CAUSE A LITTLE BLOW, JUS
WONT DO!
I NEEDED MO AND MO TO HEP ME MAKE IT THRU
AND IN TIME, I FORGOT WHAT I WUS TRY"N TO FURGET
AND, IT SEEMS YEARS NOW AH BEN LIV'N IN DIS RAGGIDY OLE TENT
YEAH, ITS BEN YEARS AND AH CAN'T REMEMB'A DA LAST TIME I HAD TO PAY
RENT
SOM TIME BACK, THEY PUT ME OUT ON THE STREET
AH DON'T WORRY BOUT MOST STUFF…JUS GETTING' SOMTHIN TO EAT
WE AIN'T BAD, YA UNDERSTAN, WE JUS TRYIN TO MAKE IT ThRU
AH SEE YOU STRAIGHTS COME DOWN HERE FOR SOME HOMO ACTION OR TO
GET SOME BLOW..YOU KNOW WHAT Y'ALL DO
TIME DUN TRULY WUNDED ALL OF US HEELS
WE'RE EVERWHERE YOU SEE, AN WE AIN'T GOT NO WHEELS
I BET IT WONT TAKE NO MORE THAN TWO GEN'RATIONS MO
FUR THE POVERTY RATE TO MOVE UP TO BOUT FORTY PERCENT, OR MAYBE
EVEN MO
SO, DON'T LOOK DOWN YUR NOSE WHEN YUR CONFRONTED WID ME
I MIGHT SLEEP IN YUR CAR, ON YUR PORCH, OR JUST COME THRU YUR WINDA
OR DOUGH
YOU KNOW IT AIN'T BUT 5000 COPS IN L.A. WATCHING TWO MILLION OR MO!
IT-A-BE JUS A FUNCTION OF TIME
THEN, WE'LL ALL BE THE SAME

NAW, I AIN'T GOT NO POLISH, GOOD ANGLISH, OR SHAME
CAUSE I'M A PRODUCT OF THIS 21ST CENTURY, LIV'IN IN A GOD-LESS COUNTRY
WID ONLY OURSELVES TO BLAME

SCREAMING WHISPERS

Mighty Strident polices the world, and gathers abundance to go to the moon
But, sooner than later, the flag unfurls and its influence and might takes a worldwide swoon

Forty million without health care; twenty percent of Hispanic households earn less than $23,000
working the whole year
Eighty-seven percent minorities fill UP the prisons
So, the obvious conclusion is abundantly clear

Our over-taxed support soon starts to pale
But they say, our economy's highly at-risk, and these duping entities are "just toO big to fail"

The "house" and the "senate" boast of a new non-partisanship
While the system's design suggests social welfare dominates, so why do they trip

How will we know when we've gone too far?
NINE hundred billion spread around so far,
And "big member" says they need government help selling us a car

"for the good of the country..... to protect the system", they say
but the "publicans" disagree, and many of the "r" people flatly refuse to play

what? NOW THE MOTHER OF ALL BAILOUTS, SEVEN HUNDRED BILLION THEY SEEK
AND, WHAT'S MORE THEY PUSH AN INATTENTIVE CONGRESS TO GET IT DONE IN
A WEEK

THE BARBAR SHOP CONTINGENT, ASKS "DID YOU SEE THE $1.4 TRILLION STOCK
MARKET LOST, DONE IN JUST ONE DAY?
fORMER EMPEROR, SENIOR TWIG, CONCLUDES THIS WILL LOOK LIKE "CHUMP
CHANGE" IF WE DON'T DO IT HIS WAY!

THIS TWO PARTY SYSTEM HAS AN EIGHT HUNDRED POUND GORILLA SITTING IN
THE ROOM
AND, HE SAYS, I ALLOWED YOU NEARLY TEN YEARS OF UNABATED SPECULATION
AND UNREGULATED BOOM

NOW, SOMEONE HAS TO PAY FOR THE $60 BILLION IN HEDGE FUND BONUSES,
GOLDEN PARACHUTES, AND OBSCENE PAY RATES FOR THE MANY CEO'S

NO TIME TO APOLOGIZE TO "JOE SIX-PACK", THE MARGINALIZED MINORITIES, OR ALL THOSE NEGATIVELY AFFECTED AS MIGHTY STRIDENT CONTINUES TO STEP ON THEIR TOES

AFFLUENCY SEEMS TO HAVE A CLICHÉ RESTRICTION AND IT'S PLAIN TO SEE THERE'S NO PLACE AT THE TOP FOR ALL THE POOR, DISENFRANCHISED FOLKS STRIVING TO BECOME ECONOMICALLY FREE.

APHORISMS 4U 2009

ONE GOD!
ONE CHURCH!
ONE CONGREGATION!

"IF MY PEOPLE THAT ARE CALLED BY <u>MY NAME</u> WOULD HUMBLE THEMSELVES AND PRAY AND SEEK <u>MY FACE</u> ….."

BIBLE-BASED TEACHING, AND SERMONS FROM "THE WORD" WHICH ARE HIGHLIGHTED AND TAUGHT "IN CONTEXT" – PRESENTED BY A SINCERE MINISTER IS SUGGESTED TO BE THE CRITERIA FOR AN "INVITATION" TO PERMIT A FELLOW CHRISTIAN PREACHER TO STAND BEFORE THE "HOME CHURCH" CONGREGATION.

BUT, MORE OFTEN THAN NOT, IN MANY OF OUR CHURCHES, A CHARISMATIC, POLISHED SPEAKER FROM "OUT OF TOWN" IS NOTED TO BE SELECTED. THE PRACTICE HINTS AT A LATENT FEAR, ESPECIALLY AMONG THE SMALLER CHURCHES, TO AVOID "MEMBER HOPING" OR EXPOSURE TO A "LOCAL" PURVEYOR OF THE "WORD" LEST THEY LOSE KEY TITHERS OR A MEMBER OF THE "FAITHFUL FEW" WHO IS "DEEMED TO BE PART OF THE "INNER CIRCLE" OF KEY MANAGEMENT OR MINISTRY LEADERSHIP WITHIN THE CHURCH.

THANK GOD FOR THOSE "HOUSES OF WORSHIP" WITH A DIFFERING PHILOSOPHY THAT BELIEVES THAT IF THE PREACHER IS "BIBLE-BASED" AND CAN TEACH AS WELL AS HE/SHE CAN PREACH, THEY ARE WELCOME!

THE BIBLICAL MANDATE OF "ONE BODY OF CHRIST" WORSHIPING IN FELLOWSHIP AND UNIFIED IN OBJECTIVES (i.e. THE "GREAT COMMISSION") IS NOT LOST.

THOUGH SOME CHURCHES INTENTIONAL FOLLOW THAT OFTEN HISTORICALLY BASED, FRAGMENTATION AND DIVISIVE SEGMENTATION OF THE CHURCHES BY SIMPLY IGNORING THE SURROUNDING HOUSES OF WORSHIP AND OPERATE WITHIN THEIR OWN LOCAL AREA.

THIS IS NO SMALL MATTER, BECAUSE THE CONSEQUENCES OF THIS CHOICE WHICH OFTEN DISGUISES A LEVEL OF ARROGANT THAT HAS FAR REACHING IMPLICATIONS.

SYSTEMS HAVE TO BE CREATED IN EACH LOCATION, UNIFIED ACTION BY "THE BODY" ARE HAMPERED, AND THE SELF PROCLAIMED "BISHOP", "APOSTLE", ETC, RESIGNS HIMSELF TO "COMPETE" WITH NEIGHBORING CONGREGATIONS AND MAY INADVERTANTLY RESORTS TO "ENTERTAINMENT, "ITCHING EAR" (GOOD NEWS ONLY!) PREACHING, OR WORST – PUT THEIR OWN "SPIN" ON INTERPRETING THE BIBLE.

WIDESPREAD LEADERSHIP PERCEPTIONS AND METHODS THEREFORE MUST CHANGE IN ORDER FOR THE "REAL AND "QUINTESSENTIAL" OR TRUE

FORMATION OF THE "BODY OF CHRIST" TO EMERGE <u>AS A SINGLE ENTITY</u> – CONNECTED BY STRENGHTENED BELIEFS AND PRACTICES WHICH ARE SHOWN IN WORSHIP, FELLOWSHIP, AND MOST IMPORTANTLY THE SHARING OF CHRIST'S VALUABLE RESOURCE… CHRISTIAN BELIEVERS.

IT'S TIME!

───────────⚜───────────

THE SPIRIT GRIEVES
AS THEY CONTINUE TO DECEIVE
THEY HAVE FORGOTTEN YOUR SOVEREIGN POWER
AS THEY TURN AWAY, AND PUT GOD ON THE SHELF
BUT, THEY KNOW
THEY ARE ONLY DECEIVING THEMSELVES

AS THE TIME OF LIFE COMES TO AN END
THEY REMAIN RECALCITRANT, AND REFUSE TO BEND
BUT DEATH'S ONSLAUGHT SOON OVERWHELMS
AND IN THOSE LAST CONSCIOUS MOMENTS
THEY ADMIT QUIETLY TO THEMSELVES

THERE'S DIVINE ORDER IN THE UNIVERSE
AND IT IS GOD THAT HAS MADE US
AND NOT WE OURSELVES

APHORISMS OF EDINGTON

- ODE TO YOUTH -

ONE COULD SAY, "WE ALL FALL PREY TO THAT "INTRACTABLE CONONDRUM"
CALLED TIME
OR, ONE COULD JUST BLURT OUT…"STOP WASTEING YOUR LIVES!"
NIHILISM AS A LIFESTYLE DICTATES GETTING HIGH, THINKING ONLY OF
ENJOYMENT, SHUNNING SACRIFICE, LONG SUFFERING OR PLAIN OLD "HARD
WORK"
HARVEY FIRESTONE ONCE REMARKED, "THE CHIEF PURPOSE OF AN
EDUCATION IS TO TRAIN THE WILL AND THE MIND TO DO WHAT MUST BE
DONE, WHEN IT MUST BE DONE, WHETHER WE WANT TO OR NOT."

NOBLE AIMS, PRAISEWORTHY MANTRAS, AND GOOD INTENTIONS SHOULD
COUNT FOR SOMETHING.
BUT, AS THE GOOD SISTER SAID, "YOU'LL KNOW WHAT I BELIEVE BY WHAT
I DO!"
PRIORITIES OF PRAGMATISM THROUGH CONSCIENTIOUS EFFORT OR
SUBCONSCIENTIOUS DESIRE WILL MORE OFTEN THAN NOT, REAR ITS UGLY
HEAD.

ARE WE SLAVES TO THE FLESH?
OR, ARE WE DISCIPLINED ENOUGH TO WIN THE OFTEN OVERWHELMING
BATTLE OF SUBJECTING OUR THOUGHTS TO THE WILL OF A HIGHER LEVEL
OF YEARNING?

WHAT A WRETCHED MAN I AM.
WHAT WILL SAVE ME FROM THE EVIL THAT I DO?

EDINGTON'S APHORISMS 4U

THE LAST HUMAN HURDLE: OLD AGE

Old Father Time is'a pickin my pocket
And I can't stop it!

Political billows may roll, Economic breakers may dash
Once my constant and ever present fear was "not enough cash!"

Life's s true Inspiration lies beyond the material
Just ask those that are "low sick", their cry is "get closer to Israel"

Lusting after the Flesh and chasing the allusive Status Quo
When it comes time for that life-ending sleep; Where does it all go?

Yes, as our mentor once said, "I've learned to live in plenty, and I've learned to live with nought
Think, where all the "stuff" finally winds up that you bought!

Like you, all that we see returns to the dust
That whimsical vapor call "Life" where is the Essence of us?

The opinion of Solomon is that "All is Vanity" as we search out our Place
Both the Good Folk and the Bad Folk wind up in the same place

Emerson asserts that we must make our lives "Sublime"
And, leave some footprint on the "Sands of Time"

But one Truism shines through our personal philosophy and will
The vernacular often sites, "Time wounds all heels"

So, play fair and keep your integrity in tact
Search out religion and know you only get once to run around Life's Track

Is the Legacy reflected in the Lives you've influenced and Their accepted choices to avoid inner shame
As succeeding generations elect your life choices though they don't even remember your name

EDINGTON'S APHORISMS4U @

SUENOS

CUANDO HAY NADA MAS DENTRO DE TI
HAY NADA MAS HACES TU
ENTOUNCES, SACA DESDE LOS SUENOS DENTRO DE TI

EL SENOR DICE ESTE ES VERDAD
CUANDO HAY NADA MAS HACES TU
TU DEBES SACAR DESDE LOS SUENOS DENTRO DE TI

CUANDO RIQUEZAS NO ES BASTANTE
Y SUS AMIGOS CON CERCA DE TI
PERO, OTROS COSAS SON NECESITAN ASISMISMO
TU DEBES SACAR DESDE LOS SUENOS DENTRO DE TI

PERO, SI ESTA LA VIDA DENTRO DE TI
TU DEBES USARLO A PROSEQUIR
PORQUE LA VIDA HACE MAS VIDA DENTRO DE TI
Y TU DEBES USARLO A PROSEQUIR

AMISTAD Y AMOR SON LA VIDA DENTRO DE TI
SON TODO DEBES TENER A PROSEQUIR

PERO, SIN AMISTAD O AMOR DENTRO DE TI
HAY NADA MAS HACES TU
SOLO SACA DESDE EL SUENO DENTRO DE TI

ENTOUNCES, CUAL QUIERES TU
LA VIDA O NADA MAS DENTRO DE TI?

EDINGTON'S APHORISMS4U

45

DREAMS

When there's nothing else inside of you
And, there's nothing else that you can do
But draw from the dreams that's inside of you

All say this is true
When there's nothing else for you to do
You must draw from the dreams inside of you

When abundance won't see you through
When friends are close to you
But, something else is still needed too
You must draw from the dreams inside of you

BUT IF LIFE IS INSIDE OF YOU
YOU MUST USE IT TO SEE YOU THROUGH
FOR LIFE BEGETS LIFE IN YOU
AND, YOU MUST USE IT TO SEE YOU THROUGH

COMPASSION IS THE LIFE THAT'S INSIDE OF YOU
IT'S ALL YOU NEED TO SEE YOU THROUGH

SO, WITHOUT LIFE'S COMPASSION INSIDE OF YOU
THERE'S NOTHING ELSE THAT YOU CAN DO
BUT DRAW FROM THE DREAMS THAT'S INSIDE OF YOU

WHICH CHOICE THEN IS THERE FOR YOU
LIFE, OR NOTHING ELSE INSIDE OF YOU

EDINGTON'S APHORISMS4U

'NIGGA PLEASE!"

Natily clad an' considered "Bad"
But his sham is but a cruel hoax
'cause when it comes time to pay
All pookie can say is, "Man, that nigga's broke!"

Wolf tickets are his way of life
Who wants reality to handle strife
But, the Kid's been reading his "dream book"
He's often heard to say, "ain't no way I can be took!"

Woe unto men of low ambition
Lacking enthusiasm and searching for illusive intuition
Camouflaging their lack of intellect
With mood swings, loud cussing, and irrelevant supestitution

But the Queens can tell if the nigga is jive, and full of it
When asked about his car, cash reserves, and health care
He's quickly busted and shown to be full of shit!

But sista girl steps off and continues her quest
Soon, she figures that the few good men are taken
And she can't use the rest

But, she keeps her a "Bubba" jus for a toy
As she starts to listen to the overtures of a new White boy.

EDINGTON'S APHORISMS4U

47

THE HAITIAN LAMENT

LIFE HERE IN HAITI IS HARD!
BUT, COMPARED TO WHAT?
HERE LIFE IS ALWAYS "HARD" OR "HARDER"
SOMETHING SEEMS TO ALWAYS DISRUPT, RAVISH, AND LAND US IN A NEW RUT

WHILE LIVING IN IMPORTED TENTS JUST TO SUSTAIN
NOW COME TORENTIAL RAINS, HIGH WINDS, AND A FULL BLOWN HURRICANE!

THE POLITICIANS SKIM THE MEAGER AID AND LEAVE THE PEOPLE BARE
WHILE THE WORLD GETS A PICTURE OF A DESTITUTE PEOPLE AND A SPIRIT
OF TOTAL DESPAIR

BUT WE LIVE IT AND SEE IT EVERY DAY
THE BENIGN NEGLECT, RAMPANT SICKNESS, AND WIDESPREAD DECAY

WE PETITION OUR GOD, WE KNOW HE'S STILL ON THE THRONE
HE PROMISED TO NEVER FORSAKE OR LEAVE US ALONE

THROUGH OUR ENDLESS SUPPLICATION AND REVERBERATING PRAYERS, HE
WILL BLESS US, AND THIS TOO SHALL PASS
FOR WE KNOW THAT ONLY MALADIES COMMON TO MAN WILL BESET US AND
THIS LATEST RANCOR WILL FADE, IT WON'T LAST

OUR SOLACE AND INDOMITABLE SPIRIT IS ELEVATED FOR WE ALL CLEARLY
KNOW WHY!
OUR JOY AND DELIVERANCE WILL COME SOON IF WE HOLD THROUGH THIS STRESS
THEN WE WILL SLEEP 'TIL RESURRECTION AS WE ENTER GOD'S PEACE AND
ETERNAL REST

APHORISMS4U

Where Do They Go?

Grandpa has gone to live with God
But mommy says, we'll see him again
She told me he's where the sun always shines and the singing never ends
And, Jesus, and the angels, and a lot of kin folks are there, up in Heaven

Sometimes I think I can see it in my mind
There are no "owwies" or hurt, but only Happy Times
One of my friends in school has gone to live there too
She was sick for a while, but now lives way up in the blue
Where the clouds are the sidewalk, and angels fly all around you

Mommy said God gives you a report card, at the end of your life
And, all the good things you do go on a long list
And, only Jesus can see it
Cause, God keeps it in his fists

I don't like to think about going away
I don't like grownups talking about Judgement day
But, my Sunday school teacher said, only bad people should be scared when they hear that kind of talk
Cause, their list is short, and they need a better "Christian walk"

I make more friends when I treat people right, and try to share
I know mommy likes it when I try to be fair
She says, God smiles, and writes a plus on my list
When I keep doing good, and ask Him to care

EDINGTON'S APHORISMS4U

PROFILE OF BLACK AMERICANS

PART - III

PROFILE OF BLACK AMERICA

"IF WE COULD KNOW **WHERE** WE ARE, AND **WHITHER** WE ARE TENDING, WE COULD THEN BETTER JUDGE **WHAT** TO DO, AND **HOW** TO DO IT"

ABE LINCOLN 1858

FOREWORD

THIS TREATESE IS NOT A POLITICAL DIATRIBE OR A PROMOTING OR PROSELYTIZING PAPER TO INITIATE VIOLENCE OR CONTRIBUTE TO A RACIAL DIVIDE.

THE FACTUAL DATA UTILIZED HEREIN REFLECT STATISTICAL INFORMATION READILY AVAILABLE IN LIBRARIES, INTERNET BLOGS, AND HISTORY BOOKS. THE BASIC MOTIVATION FOR THIS COMPOSURE IS TO BRING AWARENESS TO THE ONE HUNDRED AND FIFTY YEAR <u>HISTORICAL PERSPECTIVE</u>, <u>TREATMENT, AND REACTION</u> OF A MAJOR SEGMENT OF THE UNITED STATES OF AMERICA POPULUS- THE AFRICAN AMERICAN.

WE AT THE COVENANT COMMUNITY CHARITY BELIEVE IN BIBLICAL DOCTRINES AND RELIGIOUS GUIDANCE PROCLAMATIONS…………..SOME OF WHICH, ARE THE FOLLOWING:

"MY PEOPLE PERISH FROM LACK OF KNOWLEDGE"
HOSEA 3:6

"YOU ARE A CHOSEN PEOPLE, A ROYAL PRIESTHOOD, A HOLY NATION, A PEOPLE BELONGING TO GOD, THAT YOU MAY DECLARE THE PRAISES OF HIM WHO CALLED YOU OUT OF DARKNESS INTO HIS WONDERFUL LIGHT. ONCE YOU WERE NOT A PEOPLE, BUT NOW YOU ARE THE PEOPLE OF GOD, ONCE YOU HAD NOT RECEIVED MERCY, BUT NOW YOU HAVE RECEIVED MERCY."

"LIVE SUCH GOOD LIVES, AMONG THE PAGANS THAT, THOUGH THEY ACCUSE YOU OF DOING WRONG, THEY MAY SEE YOUR GOOD DEEDS AND GLORIFY GOD ON THE DAY HE VISITS US."
I PETER 2: 9-12

"Democratic government covers the surface of society with a network of small complicated rules, minute and uniform, through which the most original minds and the most energetic characters cannot penetrate to rise above the crowd.. The will of man is not shattered but softened, bent, and guided; men are seldom forced by it to act, but they are constantly restrained from acting. Such a power does not destroy, but it prevents existence; it does not tyrannize, but it compresses, enervates, extinguishes, and stupefies a people, till each nation is reduced to nothing better than a flock of timid and industrious animals, of which the government is the Shepard."
ALEXIS DE TOCQUEVILLE (DEMOCRACY IN AMERICA) 1862

MEMO

THE MARGINALIZED MANY AND THE HEAVY LADEN

FROM:

SOLACE AND REAL STRENGTH

IT TAKES A VERY POWERFUL PERSON NOT TO ACT IMPULSIVELY AND GET PULLED DEEPER INTO A DISASTEROUS SITUATION. IT TAKES SELF COMPOSURE AND CALM JUDGEMENT NOT TO ANSWER FALSE ACCUSATIONS, NOT TO DEFEND AGAINST INJUSTICE, OR TO FEND WITH AN "EYE FOR AN EYE" MENTALITY.

BECAUSE TO THE INSTINCTIVE HUMAN PSYCHE NOT TO ACTIVELY DEFEND ONESELF AGAINST INJUSTICE IS CONSIDERED "PASSIVE"

NOTHING COULD BE FURTHER FROM THE TRUTH!

FATHER TIME

PROFILE OF BLACK AMERICA

A STATISTICAL ANALYSIS

PREPARED BY: THE COVENANT COMMUNITY CHARITY, INC

I. GENERAL BACKGROUND

THE POPULATION OF AMERICA PER THE 2012 CENSUS BUREAU IS THREE HUNDRED AND FOURTEEN MILLION PEOPLE, OF WHICH FOURTEEN PERCENT, OR FORTY-FOUR AND A HALF MILLION ARE BLACK. THIS MEANS THAT ONE OUT OF EVERY 7 PEOPLE IN THE U.S. IS BLACK.

EIGHTY-EIGHT PERCENT OF ALL BLACKS IN THE U.S. ARE IN NINETEEN STATES (SEE CHART BELOW).

STATE	BLACK POPULATION	PERCENT OF STATE
NEW YORK	3.6 MILLION	19%
TEXAS	3.4 MILLION	13%
FLORIDA	3.4 MILLION	18%
GEORGIA	3.2 MILLION	32%
CALIFORNIA	2.9 MILLION	8%
N. CAROLINA	2.2 MILLION	23%
ILLINOIS	2.0 MILLION	16%
MARYLAND	1.8 MILLION	32%
VIRGINIA	1.7 MILLION	21%
LOUISIANA	1.5 MILLION	33%
S. CAROLINA	1.4 MILLION	29%

ALABAMA	1.3 MILLION	27%
OHIO	1.5 MILLION	14%
TENNESSEE	1.2 MILLION	18%
MISSISSIPPI	1.1 MILLION	38%
MISSOURI	763,966	13%

(19 STATES)… 39.2 MILLION 88% OF BLACKS

======================================

THE DEMOGRAPHICS WHERE BLACKS ARE LOCATED VARYS, FROM 32% OF GEORGIA'S TOTAL POPULATION; NEARLY ONE-QUARTER OF NORTH CAROLINA'S CITIZENS; ONE-THIRD OF LOUSIANIA'S POPULUS; TO AS HIGH AS ONE HALF OF THE DISTRICT OF COLUMBIA'S POPULATION ARE BLACK.

CALIFORNIA, OFTEN TOUTED AS THE THIRTEENTH WEALTHIST ENTITY IN THE WORLD, CONSISTS OF 2.9 MILLION BLACKS.

II. BLACKS & POVERTY

PER 2009 STATISTICS, 43.6 MILLION AMERICANS ARE LIVING IN POVERTY. THE OFFICIAL INCOME THRESHOLD IS $21,756 PER ANNUM. THIS EQUATES TO $418 PER WEEK – WHILE A FORTY HOUR WORK WEEK YIELDS ABOUT $10 PER HOUR OF "GROSS" EARNINGS.

9.9 MILLION BLACKS IN AMERICA OR ROUGHLY - ONE IN FIVE AFRICAN AMERICANS- LIVE IN POVERTY. THE UNEMPLOYMENT RATE FOR BLACKS IN AMERICA IS 16% OF THE TOTAL UNEMPLOYMENT STATISTICS. HOWEVER, ONLY PERSONS THAT ARE ACTIVELY SEEKING EMPLOYMENT ARE COUNTED IN THAT RATE.

APPROXIMATELY, 11.5% OF AFRICAN AMERICANS (ABOUT 5 MILLION, OR ONE IN NINE) LIVE IN GOVERNMENT HOUSING OR ARE RECEIVING "SECTION-8" HOUSING SUBSIDY; WHILE 13.6% (ABOUT 6 MILLION, OR ONE IN EIGHT) ARE RECEIVING WELFARE CHECKS; 25% OF AFRICAN AMERICANS (OVER ELEVEN MILLION OR ONE IN FOUR) ARE RECEIVING FOOD STAMPS.

II. EMPLOYMENT AND BUSINESS

AFRICAN AMERICANS HAVE AN UNEMPLOYMENT RATE ALMOST DOUBLE THAT OF THE OVERALL POPULATION. THE FEDERAL GOVERNMENT WAS ONE OF THE FIRST TO INTEGRATE. THUS, FIFTY YEARS LATER, AFRICAN AMERICANS ARE OVER-REPRESENTED IN THAT WORK SECTOR. ONE IN FIVE, OR 20%, OF U.S. BLACKS OVER 16 YEARS OF AGE ARE EMPLOYEES OF THE FEDERAL, STATE OR LOCAL GOVERNMENT.

LESS THAN 4% OF AFRICAN AMERICANS ARE SELF-EMPLOYED. IT SHOULD BE NOTED THAT 94% OF SELF-EMPLOYED BLACKS HAVE NO EMPLOYEES.

THE LONG HONORED BIAS OF BLACK FEMALES INTEGRATING INTO SOCIETY'S WORK FORCE AT A DISPROPORTIONATE RATE AHEAD OF BLACK MEN IS STILL NOTED. IN 2011, 33% OF EMPLOYED BLACK WOMEN HAVE JOBS IN MANAGEMENT OR PROFESSIONAL OCCUPATIONS.

THIRTY-SIX PERCENT OF BLACK MEN, ON THE OTHER HAND, HAVE "BLUE COLLAR" OCCUPATIONS.

III. POLITICAL PARTY AFFILIATION

AFTER THE CIVIL WAR, ALMOST ALL BLACKS CONSIDERED THEMSELVES REPUBLICANS. IT WAS ABRAHAM LINCOLN'S ABOLITIONIST PARTY WHICH PROMOTED AN END TO SLAVERY. BUT, SOUTHERN DEMOCRATS STRONGLY OPPOSED ANY RIGHTS FOR BLACKS AND FOR ALMOST A CENTURY THEREAFTER AFRICAN AMERICANS WERE NOT EVEN ALLOWED TO OFFICIALLY ATTEND THE DEMOCRATIC CONVENTION UNTIL 1924. (NOTE: "1924" THIS DISENFRANCHISEMENT OCCURRED BOTH DURING AND AFTER WORLD WAR ONE – WHERE THOUSANDS OF BLACKS WERE KILLED OR INJURED WHILE SERVING IN A SEGREGATED MILITARY)

IN 2004, 67% OF AFRICAN AMERICANS WERE AFFILIATED WITH THE DEMOCRATIC PARTY; 11% WERE "INDEPENDENTS- NEAR DEMOCRATS"; 13% WERE INDEPENDENTS;WHILE APPROXIMATELY

8% WERE "INDEPENDENTS-NEAR REPUBLICANS"

THE MAJOR SHIFT OCCURRED AFTER THE 1964 CIVIL RIGHTS LEGISLATION OUTLAWING DISCRIMINATION AND THE 1965 VOTING RIGHTS LEGISLATION PROMOTED BY PRESIDENTS KENNEDY AND JOHNSON.

OVER THE LAST FORTY YEARS AFRICAN AMERICANS HAVE CONSISTENTLY VOTED OVERWHELMINGLY FOR DEMOCRATIC PRESIDENTIAL CANDIDATES.

THE MOST VOTES ANY REPUBLICAN CANDIDATE RECEIVED FROM BLACKS SINCE 1968 WAS GERALD FORD (15%).

IN THE 2008 ELECTIONS 97% OF BLACKS VOTED FOR THE DEMOCRATIC CANDIDATE, BARAK OBAMA.

IV. THE BLACK CHURCH

IN 2007, THE "RELIGIOUS LANDSCAPE SURVEY" CONDUCTED BY THE PEW FOUNDATION, DISCLOSED THAT 87% OF AFRICAN AMERICANS ARE AFFILIATED WITH A RELIGION.

IT WAS FOUND THAT 79% OF BLACKS (VERSUS 56% OVERALL) INDICATED THAT RELIGION IS "VERY IMPORTANT IN THEIR LIFE".

RELIGIOUS AFFILIATIONS OF AFRICAN AMERICANS

BAPTIST 45%
PENTECOSTAL 8%
PROTESTANT 7%
METHODIST 5%
NONDENOMINATION 5%
CATHOLIC 5%
JEW, HINDU, BUDDIST ... 4%
JEHOVAH WITNESS,
MUSLIM, HOLINESS 7%
NON-RELIGIOUS 12%

TODAY, 83% OF AFRICAN AMERICANS ARE "CHRISTIANS" IN ONE DENOMINATION/AFFILIATION OR ANOTHER, AND ONLY 1% IDENTIFY THEMSELVES AS MUSLIM.

REGARDING CHURCH ATTENDANCE: 61% OF AFRICAN AMERICAN WOMEN ATTEND CHURCH EITHER WEEKLY OR AT LEAST ONCE A MONTH; WHEREAS, 47% OF BLACK MEN ATTEND CHURCH AT THAT RATE; 28% OF BLACK MEN ATTEND CHURCH LESS THAN ONCE A YEAR OR NEVER.

V. STOPPED, SEARCHED AND ARRESTED

EVERY FEW YEARS A NATIONAL INCIDENT OCCURS IN THE BLACK COMMUNITY WHERE A BLACK MAN IS HANDLED WITH EXCESSIVE FORCE OR IS SHOT TO DEATH BY POLICE.

THE CONFRONTATION MAY BE TAPED OR DUE TO THE SURROUNDING CIRCUMSTANCES THE AFRICAN AMERICAN COMMUNITY AND SOMETIMES THE MEDIA WILL RALLY BEHIND THE ALLEGED VICTIM AND DEMAND JUSTICE.

WHEN THIS OCCURS THE AGE-OLD QUESTION RESURFACES ABOUT WHETHER OR NOT BLACK MEN ARE UNFAIRLY TARGETED BY LAW ENFORCEMENT.

IN 2005, THE "BUREAU OF JUSTICE STATISTICS" RELEASED A REPORT CONSISTING OF 80,000 AMERICANS REGARDING TRAFFIC STOPS AND THE CIRCUMSTANCES SURROUNDING CONTACT WITH THE POLICE. THE REPORT FOUND:

9% OF WHITE DRIVERS WERE STOPPED
9% OF BLACK DRIVERS WERE STOPPED
9% OF HISPANIC DRIVERS WERE STOPPED

THE VARIANCE IN TREATMENT APPEARS TO OCCUR "AFTER THE STOP".

AFRICAN AMERICANS AND HISPANICS WERE MUCH LESS LIKELY TO BE ISSUED A SIMPLE TRAFFIC WARNING FROM POLICE AS OFTEN HAPPENED WITH THEIR WHITE COUNTERPART.

AFRICAN AMERICANS AND HISPANICS WERE THREE TIMES MORE LIKELY TO BE "SEARCHED"; MORE THAN THREE TIMES MORE LIKELY TO BE "HANDCUFFED", AND ALMOST THREE TIMES MORE LIKELY TO BE "ARRESTED".

UNEQUAL TREATMENT WAS ALSO NOTED IN ANOTHER JUSTICE DEPT. REPORT THAT DISCLOSED THAT 9% OF THE BLACKS THAT WERE NOT ARRESTED WERE SEARCHED, WHEREAS ONLY 3% OF THE WHITES STOPPED BUT NOT ARRESTED WERE SEARCHED.

AT 2009, ACCORDING TO THE DEPT OF JUSTICE, AFRICAN AMERICANS SENTENCES FOR "DRUG" CONVICTIONS (OF MORE THAN ONE YEAR) IN STATE PRISONS OCCURS MORE THAN ANY OTHER OFFENSE. APPROXIMATELY, 122,600 BLACKS WERE UNDER STATE JURISDICTION FOR DRUGS-RELATED OFFENSES, THUS, 21.1% (OVER ONE IN FIVE) OF ALL BLACK STATE INMATES ARE IMPRISONED FOR DRUG-RELATED ARRESTS.

THE TABLE BELOW INDICATES THE TOTAL STATE, FEDERAL AND LOCAL INCARCERATION NUMBERS (IN 2010, FOR MEN).

YEAR	BLACK	WHITE	HISPANIC	OTHER	TOTAL
STATE/FED'L					
2010	561,400	451,600	327,200	105,800	1,446,000
LOCAL JAILS					
2010	283,200	331,600	118,100	15,000	748,728
TOTAL	**844,600**	**783,200**	**445,300**	**120,800**	**2,194,728**

VI. SUMMATION

IN THE ONE HUNDRED AND FIFTY YEARS SINCE THE CIVIL WAR, AFRICAN AMERICANS HAVE WITHSTOOD SEEMINGLY ENDLESS SOCIETAL ASSAULTS ON THEIR "LIFE, LIBERTY AND PURSUIT OF HAPPINESS".

HISTORICALLY, THEY WERE INITIALLY DEEMED BY THE OFFICIAL "COURT OF THE LAND" AS "CHATTEL" OR PROPERTY, AND THE PROGRESSION TO FULL CITIZENSHIP WAS EFFECTIVELY STOPPED BY THE "DIXIECRATS" OR SOUTHERN DEMOCRATS FOR APPROXIMATELY SEVENTY ADDITIONAL YEARS UNTIL WORLD WAR II ENDED WHEN POLITICIANS AND CIVIL RIGHTS GROUPS BROUGHT NATIONAL ATTENTION TO THE DISPARITIES BETWEEN THE RACES.

NATIONAL ISSUES SUCH AS BANK LOAN DISCRIMINATION AND "RED LINING", SEGREGATION IN THE MILITARY, AND LIMITED OPPORTUNITIES

FOR BLACKS WITHIN THE ARMED SERVICES TO GAIN ADEQUATE TRAINING FOR THE POST-MILITARY YEARS, LANDMARK LITIGATION FOR SEPARATE AND UNEQUAL EDUCATION OPPORTUNITIES, BARRIERS AGAINST VOTING, HOUSING DISCRIMINATION, MORTGAGE LENDING PITFALLS, EMPLOYMENT BIASES – AND, AS IF THESE OBSTACLES WERE NOT ENOUGH "ASASSINATION" ALL TOO OFTEN BROUGHT A CRIPPLING BLOW TO THE SOCIAL CHANGE MOVEMENTS.

OFTEN "CHARACTER ASASSINATIONS", IMPRISONMENT, OR EXPENSIVE DRAWN OUT LEGAL ACCUSATIONS BECAME THE UTILIZED METHOD TO SWAY PUBLIC OPINION OR SYMPATHY... DR. MARTIN LUTHER KING, MALCOM X, ADAM CLAYTON POWELL, ELIJAH MOHAMMAD, HUEY NEWTON, MOHAMMAD ALI... ARE BUT A FEW WHO WERE VICTIMIZED AND DOGGEDLY GIVEN BAD PRESS TO SHAPE NEGATIVE PUBLIC OPINION.

DEFENDING ENTITIES OFTEN IMPLIED OR LATER PROVED THAT THE GOVERNMENT ITSELF (F.B.I. OR I.R.S.) WAS THE CULPRIT BEHIND THE DISCREDITING.

GIVEN THIS HISTORICAL SCENARIO, AFRICAN AMERICANS ESPECIALLY BLACK MEN FEEL THEY HAVE A BULL'S EYE ON THEIR BACK, AND THAT THOSE PAID OR ELECTED TO "SERVE AND PROTECT" ARE OFTEN CONSIDERED "THE GANG IN BLUE".

PROLOGUE

⊹⟨⟩⫻⟨⟩⊹

THIS TREATESE IS NOT A POLITICAL DIATRIBE OR A PROMOTING OR PROSELYTIZING STUDY TO INITIATE VIOLENCE OR CONTRIBUTE TO A RACIAL DIVIDE.

THE FACTUAL DATA UTILIZED HEREIN REFLECT STATISTICAL INFORMATION READILY AVAILABLE IN LIBRARIES, INTERNET BLOGS, AND HISTORY BOOKS. THE BASIC MOTIVATION FOR THIS COMPOSURE IS TO BRING AWARENESS TO THE ONE HUNDRED AND FIFTY YEAR <u>HISTORICAL PERSPECTIVE</u>, <u>TREATMENT, AND REACTION</u> OF A MAJOR SEGMENT OF THE UNITED STATES POPULUS- THE AFRICAN AMERICAN.

WE AT THE COVENANT COMMUNITY CHARITY BELIEVE IN BIBLICAL DOCTRINES AND RELIGIOUS GUIDANCE PROCLAMATIONS…………..SOME OF WHICH, ARE THE FOLLOWING:

"MY PEOPLE PERISH FROM LACK OF KNOWLEDGE"
HOSEA 3:6

"YOU ARE A CHOSEN PEOPLE, A ROYAL PRIESTHOOD, A HOLY NATION, A PEOPLE BELONGING TO GOD, THAT YOU MAY DECLARE THE PRAISES OF HIM WHO CALLED YOU OUT OF DARKNESS INTO HIS WONDERFUL LIGHT. ONCE YOU WERE NOT A PEOPLE, BUT NOW YOU ARE THE PEOPLE OF GOD, ONCE YOU HAD NOT RECEIVED MERCY, BUT NOW YOU HAVE RECEIVED MERCY."

"LIVE SUCH GOOD LIVES, AMONG THE PAGANS THAT, THOUGH THEY ACCUSE YOU OF DOING WRONG, THEY MAY SEE YOUR GOOD DEEDS AND GLORIFY GOD ON THE DAY HE VISITS US."
I PETER 2: 9-12

"NO WEAPON FORMED AGAINST YOU SHALL PROSPER"

> "When the hour and the real cause has come, the infection flashes like an electric spark over hundreds of miles…..The message goes through the air, and, in the one thing that counts all men are suddenly of one mind even if only in a blind conviction: **things must change**."
> JACOB BURCKHARDT (1869 "THE CRISES OF HISTORY)